Enrichment

MATH & READING

Grades 1 & 2

Dear Young Learner,

Welcome to your new *Enrichment Book*. Inside, you'll find lots of fun things to do. There are games and puzzles. There are stories to write. There are riddles, contests, and even a few surprises. And best of all, you'll have the chance to share all the fun with your family or friends.

While you are having fun, you will also be learning some important math and reading skills, skills you will be able to use in school and for the rest of your life.

We know this book will be one of your favorite ways to learn-- and to have fun!

Sincerely,

Your Learning Partners at
American Education Publishing

Table of Contents
Math Grade 1

Pages

Counting and Place Value

11 My House
12 My Family
13 Hunt for Numbers
14 Can You Do It?
15 Here is Your Zoo
16 Counting Path
17 Letters, Letters, Letters
18 My Name
19 Spoons, Forks, Knives
20 Fill the Spoon
21 The Stick Family
22 Name Writing Contest
23 Circles and Squares
24 Count Up Time
25 Lots of Stars
26 Circle Them Up
27 Money Road
28 Pick Your Money Road

Addition and Subtraction

29 Dominoes
30 Target Game
31 The Color of 5
32 5 in a Bowl
33 Bug Zoo
34 Number Ladder
35 Housework
36 Emu the Robot
37 In the Box
38 10 on Plates
39 The Cover Up
40 What's Hiding
41 Hilda Hid It
42 Lose and Win Game

Pages

43 Tic-Tac-Toe
44 Tic-Tac-Toe
45 Add 10
46 Rainbow Numbers
47 Heads or Tails
48 The 77 Game

Geometry and Measurement

49 The Square Family
50 What Rolls?
51 A Shape Hunt
52 Shape Game
53 A Pencil Long
54 A Trip Across Your Room
55 Your Shoe
56 Your Hand
57 Which is Heavier?
58 Fill it Up
59 Clocks
60 My Day
61 How Tall — How Long
62 Guess How Long

Mathematical Thinking

63 Puzzle Parts
64 Numbers About Me
65 Crazy Creatures
66 Your Kitchen
67 Silly Pictures
68 Can You Find It?
69 Number Pictures
70 Pattern Page
71 Colored Boxes
72 More Colored Boxes
73 Work Sheet
74 Work Sheet
75 Work Sheet

Math Grade 2

Pages

Counting and Place Value

77 Numbers Everywhere
78 Family Matters
79 House Points
80 Make a Number
81 Catch the Sneak
82 Put Them in Order
83 100 Every Which Way
84 Number Contest
85 How Many?
86 So Many Circles
87 Count by 10
88 Odd and Even
89 Pennies and Dimes
90 Money Mats
91 Ring It
92 Hit the Number

Addition and Subtraction

93   Toss and Add
94   Tic-Tac-Toe
95   On or Off the Plate
96   4 in a Row
97   Look for Cover
98   Math Baseball
99   Mistakes All Over
100 Fill in Your Circle
101 Find the Oddball and More
102 Little Checkers
103 Make 10 Any Way You Can
104 Math Star
105 Amazing 9
106 Family Ages
107 Darts
108 A Giant Number Story

Pages

109 Calendar Math

110 Rainbow Colors

111 Words Are Worth It

112 Box Numbers

113 Adding and Subtracting Around the House

114 Pick a Number

Geometry and Measurement

115 How Long?

116 Foot Time

117 Inches and Centimeters

118 The Size of You

119 Going Around

120 The Weight of Things

121 Estimate It!

122 Which Holds More?

123 Dot to Dot

124 Hidden Shapes

125 Solid Shapes

126 Buildings

127 The Time of Day

128 Time It

Mathematical Thinking

129 Can You See It?

130 Making Squares

131 Who Is Who?

132 Estimate First

133 Fits the Bill

134 And And And

135 Hundreds of Patterns

136 Get 102

137 Space Creatures

138 What to Wear?

139 Work Sheet

140 Work Sheet

141 Work Sheet

Reading Grade 1

Readiness

143 My Clown *(visual discrimination)*

144 Is It the Same? *(visual discrimination)*

145 To the Doghouse *(eye-hand coordination)*

146 It Moved *(visual memory)*

147 Rhyme Design *(rhyming words)*

148 Orders *(auditory memory)*

149 Sounds, Sounds *(auditory discrimination)*

150 In My Home *(auditory discrimination)*

Word Skills

151 The Farm *(initial consonants)*

152 Suitcases *(initial, final consonants)*

153 Tic-Tac-Toe *(short vowels)*

154 Toss a Word *(short vowels)*

155 Word Hunt *(short vowels)*

156 Make a Word *(short vowels)*

157 Silly Drawings *(short vowels)*

158 Do They Sound the Same? *(short vowels)*

159 Word Stars *(consonant blends)*

160 Beginnings and Endings *(consonant blends)*

161 Hidden Message *(consonant digraphs)*

162 Down the Road *(consonant digraphs)*

163 They Are Hiding *(long vowels)*

164 Word Boxes *(long vowels)*

165 Who Is the Winner? *(long vowels)*

166 Word Wheel *(long vowels)*

Vocabulary

167 Like It or Not *(sight vocabulary)*

168 Word Boxes *(sight vocabulary)*

169 Label Me *(sight vocabulary)*

170 Story Words *(sight vocabulary)*

171 Zoo or Farm? *(sight vocabulary)*

172 Word Checkers *(sight vocabulary)*

173 Find the One *(related words)*

174 Which Is Better? *(related words)*

175 It's a Fact *(synonyms)*

176 Fill the Balloons *(synonyms, antonyms)*

177 A Riddle *(context clues)*

178 Lost Words *(context clues)*

Comprehension

179 Name the Pictures *(main idea)*

180 What Is Happening? *(main idea)*

181 Puppy Puppet *(following directions)*

182 Pick Up the Ice *(following directions)*

183 Work Tools *(categorizing)*

184 Fill the Lists *(categorizing)*

185 At the Zoo *(predicting outcomes)*

186 What Now? *(predicting outcomes)*

187 Party Time *(sequencing)*

188 The Right Order *(sequencing)*

189 Tim Bear *(details)*

190 Remembering *(details)*

191 Plans, Plans *(cause and effect)*

192 Why Did It Happen? *(cause of events)*

193 Name the Person *(character analysis)*

194 A Helping Hand *(character analysis)*

195 The Moon *(main idea)*

196 What's It About? *(main idea)*

197 Picture the Story *(visual images)*

198 Name the Animals *(visual images)*

Forms of Writing

199 My Favorites *(autobiography)*

200 Who Was First? *(history)*

201 Three Poems *(poetry)*

202 Our Poem *(poetry)*

203 Who Will Help? *(folk tale)*

204 After the Story Ends *(fairy tales)*

205 Work Sheet

206 Work Sheet

207 Work Sheet

Reading Grade 2

Word Skills

209 Lost Letters *(short vowels)*

210 Make a Word *(short vowels)*

211 Mystery Time *(long vowels)*

212 Is It a Word? *(long vowels)*

213 Yes or No *(vowel digraphs)*

214 Toss a Word *(vowel digraphs)*

215 Hidden Words *(consonant blends)*

216 Lotto *(consonant blends)*

217 Riddle Time *(consonant digraphs)*

218 Tongue Twisters *(consonant digraphs)*

219 Trail of Nonsense *(r-controlled vowels)*

220 Weave a Word *(r-controlled vowels)*

221 Hidden Picture *(hard and soft c)*

222 Hard or Soft? *(hard and soft g)*

223 Ink Spots *(inflectional endings)*

224 Family Matters *(comparatives)*

Vocabulary

225 Three of Everything *(sight vocabulary)*

226 Tic-Tac-Toe Words *(sight vocabulary)*

227 Word Pictures *(sight vocabulary)*

228 Word Road *(sight vocabulary)*

229 Word Hunt *(compound words)*

230 Compound Memory *(compound words)*

231 Line Designs *(contractions)*

232 Star Bright *(contractions)*

233 Pretty As a Picture *(synonyms)*

234 Touchdown *(synonyms)*

235 Find the Mistakes *(antonyms)*

236 Opposites *(antonyms)*

237 The Long Sneeze *(multiple meaning words)*

238 Riddle-De-Day *(multiple meaning words)*

239 Help the Writer *(context clues)*

240 All Mixed Up *(context clues)*

241 Draw It *(prepositions)*

242 No Sillies Allowed *(prepositional phrases)*

Comprehension

243 What's the Story *(sentences)*

244 Sentence Fun *(sentences)*

245 Who Did It? *(following directions)*

246 Make a Cat *(following directions)*

247 Vacation Time *(categories, drawing conclusions)*

248 What's the Game? *(drawing conclusions)*

249 It's a Problem *(predicting outcomes)*

250 What Next? *(predicting outcomes)*

251 Birthday Party *(sequencing)*

252 Before, During, After *(sequencing)*

253 Off to the Movies *(details)*

254 What Happened Here? *(details)*

255 Why? Why? Why? *(cause and effect)*

256 What Will Happen? *(cause and effect)*

257 Silly Nilly *(character analysis)*

258 My Friend *(character analysis)*

259 Two Young People *(main idea)*

260 Is It True? *(main idea)*

261 Follow the Plan *(story plan)*

262 Odd or Even Story *(story plan)*

Forms of Writing

263 The Truth *(nonfiction)*

264 Interview *(nonfiction)*

265 Goo or Roo? *(fantasy, reality)*

266 Could It Be? *(fantasy, reality)*

267 Poems *(poetry)*

268 Share a Wish *(poetry)*

269 A Magical Tale *(fairy tales)*

270 Fairy Tale Quiz *(fairy tales)*

271 **Work Sheet**

272 **Work Sheet**

273-288 **Answer Keys**

Enrichment
Math Grade 1

AMERICAN
EDUCATION
PUBLISHING

My House

Tell about your house.

My house has _____ beds.

My house has _____ doors.

My house has _____ bananas.

My house has _____ elephants.

My house has _____ sinks.

My Family

Draw a family picture.
Have a grown-up help you.

How many people are in your picture? _____
Have a grown-up write their names.
You write the number of letters.

Mom _____   **3** ___   _____   _____

_____   ___   _____   ___

_____   ___   _____   _____

_____   ___

Name _____   **Math Grade 1**

Hunt for Numbers

Numbers are everywhere.

Look for **3, 5, 8, 9.**

Draw pictures.   Where did you find them?

3	5
8	9

Can You Do It?

Try to do it.

Ask a grown-up to check your counting.

Draw a smile on the button if you did it.

Jump **3** times.

Take **8** big steps.

Touch your nose **6** times.

Clap your hands **15** times.

Hop **13** times.

Make **10** silly faces.

Here Is Your Zoo

Draw more elephants, snakes, birds, and monkeys in your zoo.

My zoo has _____ elephants.

My zoo has _____ snakes.

My zoo has _____ monkeys.

My zoo has _____ birds.

Counting Path

Play this game with a grown-up.
You need a coin.

1. Put the coin on START.

2. Take turns moving the coin on the path.
You can move 1, 2, or 3 spaces.

3. The person who gets the coin to FINISH wins.

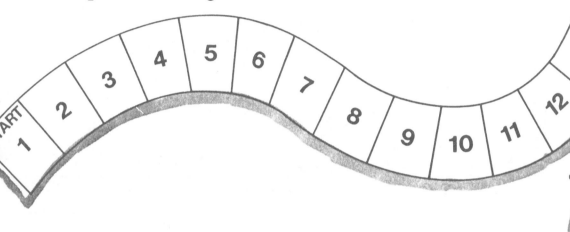

Who won? _____

Play again.

Who won? _____

Make your own number path.
Make it longer. Make it go to **20** or more.
Play the game on your path.

Letters, Letters, Letters

You can count letters.

Count every v on this page. How many? _____

Count every y on this page. How many? _____

Count every v and every y. How many? _____

Count every w on this page. How many? _____

Count every v and every w. How many? _____

My Name

Do this with a grown-up.

My first name is _____ .

My first name has _____ letters.

My last name is _____ .

My last name has _____ letters.
Count these letters in your name.

a ____   **e** ____   **i** ____   **o** ____   **u** ____

Color a box for each **a**, **e**, **i**, **o**, and **u** in your name.

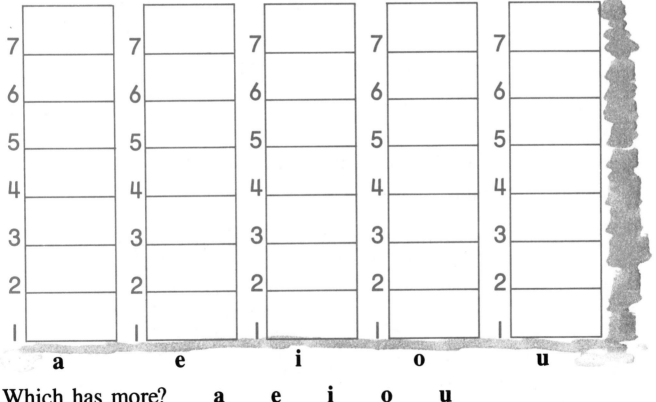

Which has more?   **a   e   i   o   u**

Counting, Graphing, and Comparing Numbers

Spoons, Forks, Knives

Count in your kitchen.

Count spoons.   Count forks.   Count knives.

_____ spoons   _____ forks   _____ knives

Ring the answer.

I have more   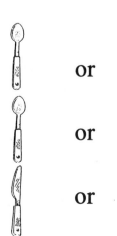   or

I have more   or   

I have more   or

Fill the Spoon

Play this with a grown-up.

You need a tablespoon.

You need a box or jar of little things, like dried beans, nuts or popcorn.

Fill the spoon with beans.

Guess how many. _____

Count how many. _____

Fill the spoon again. Try to put in even more!

Guess how many. _____

Count how many. _____

Estimating and Counting

The Stick Family

This is a stick dad.	Draw a stick mom.	Draw a stick boy.	Draw a stick girl.

The stick family has _____ feet.

The stick family has _____ eyes.

The stick family has _____ arms.

The stick family has _____ fingers.

The stick family has _____ tails.

How many are there in your family?

_____ feet _____ eyes _____ arms _____ fingers

Name Writing Contest

Do this with a grown-up.

Color the boxes with these numbers: 5, 10, 15, 20, 25, 30, 35, 40, 45, 50, 55, 60, 65, 70, 75, 80, 85, 90, 95, 100.

1	2	3	4	5	6	7	8	9	10
11	12	13	14	15	16	17	18	19	20
21	22	23	24	25	26	27	28	29	30
31	32	33	34	35	36	37	38	39	40
41	42	43	44	45	46	47	48	49	50
51	52	53	54	55	56	57	58	59	60
61	62	63	64	65	66	67	68	69	70
71	72	73	74	75	76	77	78	79	80
81	82	83	84	85	86	87	88	89	90
91	92	93	94	95	96	97	98	99	100

Do you see a pattern? _____

Have your grown-up count by fives to 100.

Write your name as often as you can while he counts.

How many times did you write your name? _____

LESSON
7

Circles and Squares

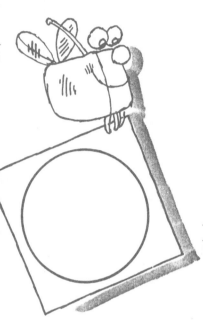

□   ○

Draw 10 squares in each circle.

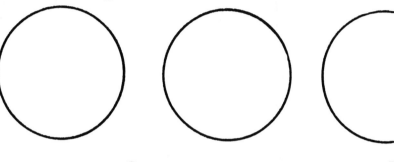

○   □

How many circles? _____   How many squares? _____

□

Draw 6 more squares here.

□

How many squares now? _____

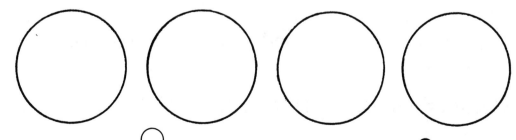

Draw 10 dots in each circle.

How many circles? _____   How many dots? _____

Count Up Time

Ask a grown-up to help you.

You need many things like dried beans or paper clips.

1	2	3	4	5	6
7	8	9	10	11	12

Put 1 bean in box 1.

Put 2 beans in box 2.

Put 3 beans in box 3, and so on up to box 12.

Count all the beans. How many in all? _____

Lots of Stars

10 stars are in a cloud.

Put 10 more in a cloud.

Put 10 more in a cloud.

Put 10 more in a cloud.

How many clouds? _____

How many stars? _____

Circle Them Up

Do this with a grown-up.

You need some little things, like dried beans or paper clips.

Count 19 beans.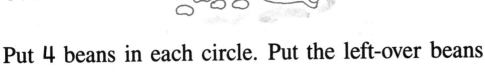

Put 4 beans in each circle. Put the left-over beans in the triangle.

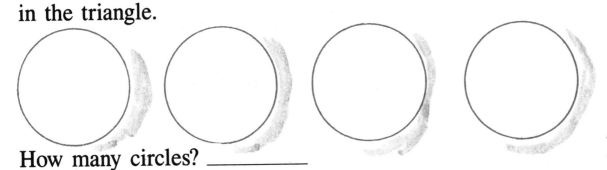

How many circles? _____

How many beans are in the triangle? _____

Do it again. This time put 10 beans in the circle.
Put the left-over beans in the triangle.

How many circles? _____

How many beans are in the triangle? _____

Grouping Numbers

Money Road

Count the money on the road.

How many cents? _____ ¢

Count the money on this road.

How many cents? _____ ¢

Count the money on this road.

How many cents? _____ ¢

Pick Your Money Road

Play this game with a grown-up.

There are 4 money roads.

Pick a road. Count the money. How many cents? _____ ¢

Your grown-up picks a road. How many cents? _____ ¢

Who got the most money? _____

Play again. Pick a different road.

Who got the most money this time? _____

Counting Money by Ones, Fives and Tens

Dominoes

How many dots in all?

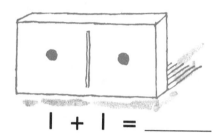

1 + 1 = _____

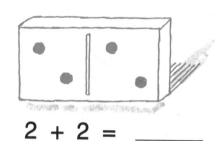

2 + 2 = _____

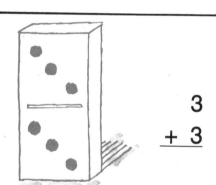

3
+ 3

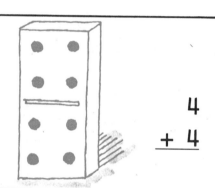

4
+ 4

4 + 4 = _____

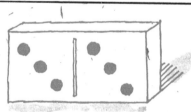

3 + 3 = _____

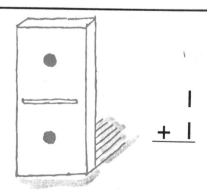

1
+ 1

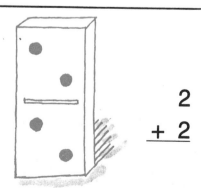

2
+ 2

Target Game

Play this game with a grown-up.

Toss a coin or a paper clip on the game board.

Write the number.

Toss again.

Write the number.

Add the numbers.

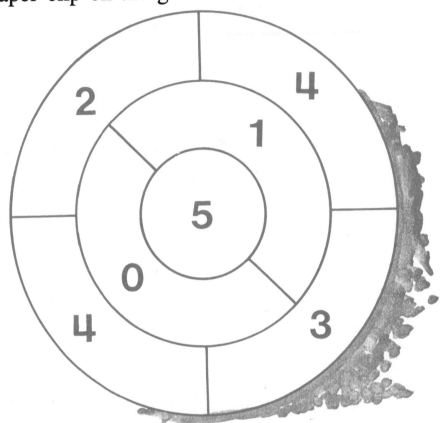

My score

Toss 1 _____

Toss 2 _____

Add up _____

My grown-up's score

Toss 1 _____

Toss 2 _____

Add up _____

Who won? _____

Play again. Who won? _____

Adding with Basic Facts: Sums to 10

LESSON
11

The Color of 5

red   blue

Get a red crayon and a blue crayon.
Color the boxes.
Color some red and some blue.
How many reds ? _____
How many blues ? _____

_____ + _____ = 5

red   blue

Color some red and some blue.

How many reds ? _____
How many blues ? _____

_____ + _____ = 5

red   blue

Color some red and some blue.

How many reds ? _____
How many blues ? _____

_____ + _____ = 5

red   blue

in a Bowl

You need **5** pennies or **5** paper clips.
You also need a bowl.
Put the bowl on the floor.
Stand away from the bowl.
Try to throw the pennies into the bowl.
Write how many go inside.
Write how many go outside.
Play **3** times.

My first time

Pennies inside _____

Pennies outside _____

My grown-up's first time

Pennies inside _____

Pennies outside _____

My second time

Pennies inside _____

Pennies outside _____

My grown-up's second time

Pennies inside _____

Pennies outside _____

My third time

Pennies inside _____

Pennies outside _____

My grown-up's third time

Pennies inside _____

Pennies outside _____

Adding with Basic Facts: Sums of 5

Bug Zoo

 □□
Here are ant boxes.

 □
Put **5** ants in each box.

How many ants in all? _____   5 + 5 = _____

 □□
Here are butterfly boxes.

 □
Put **7** butterflies in each box.

How many butterflies in all? _____ 7 + 7 = _____

 □□
Here are spider boxes.

□
Put **9** spiders in each box.

How many spiders in all? _____   9 + 9 = _____

Number Ladder

Play this game with a grown-up.

Climb the number ladder.

Start at the bottom.

Add 1 to the number on each step.

If you make a mistake, you fall.

Then you must start over.

When you make it to the top,
put a ⌣ on the

Play again. Add **2** at each step.

Play again. Add **3** at each step.

Play again. Add **4** at each step.

Ladder steps (top to bottom): 7, 9, 6, 8, 4, 0, 2, 5, 1, 3

Housework

How many sinks are in your house?
How many beds in your house?
How many in all?

_____ + _____ = _____

        in all

How many lions are in your house?
How many tigers?
How many in all?

_____ + _____ = _____

    in all

How many doors are in your house?
How many umbrellas are in your house?
How many in all?

_____ + _____ = _____

        in all

Emu the Robot

Work with a grown-up to fill in the numbers for this story.

Emu is a good robot. He has magic flowers. He has _____ magic red flowers and _____ magic blue flowers. How many magic flowers in all? _____

Emu goes for a walk. He meets _____ boys and _____ girls.

How many boys and girls in all? _____

With his magic flowers, he gives the children some birds. He gives them _____ redbirds and _____ bluebirds. How many birds in all? _____

2 birds fly away. How many birds now? _____

Emu must go home now.

He waves goodbye _____ times.

The children wave _____ times.

How many goodbye waves in all? _____

Emu walks _____ miles.

He runs _____ miles.

How many miles in all? _____

Solving Word Problems

In The Box

LESSON
14

Get some beans or other little things.

Put **2**
here.

Put **3**
here.

Put **3**
here.

Put **2**
here.

How many? _____

2 + 3 = _____

How many? _____

3 + 2 = _____

Put **4**
here.

Put **5**
here.

Put **5**
here.

Put **4**
here.

How many? _____

4 + 5 = _____

How many? _____

5 + 4 = _____

Using the Commutative Property of Addition

10 on Plates

Do this with a grown-up.

You need 10 pennies or paper clips.

You need 2 plates.

Put the 10 pennies on the 2 plates.

Here is one way to do it.   Here is another way.

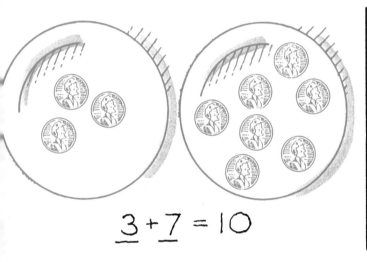 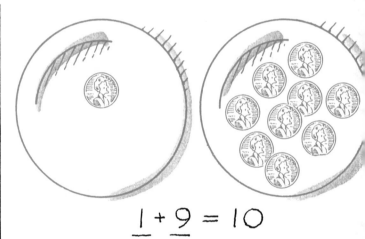

$$3 + 7 = 10$$ $$1 + 9 = 10$$

Now use your pennies and plates. Try to find 6 new ways.

Write numbers to show what you did.

_____ + _____ = 10   _____ + _____ = 10

_____ + _____ = 10   _____ + _____ = 10

_____ + _____ = 10   _____ + _____ = 10

Adding with Basic Facts: Sums of 10

The Cover Up

LESSON
15

Here are 10 circles.

Cover **2** circles. How many now? _____

Cover **8** circles. How many now? _____

Cover **6** circles. How many now? _____

Cover **4** circles. How many now? _____

Cover **3** circles. How many now? _____

Cover **7** circles. How many now? _____

Cover **5** circles. How many now? _____

What's Hiding?

Play this game with a grown-up.

You need 10 little things like beans, pennies, or paper clips.

Step 1 The grown-up puts some on a table. You count how many.

Step 2 Close your eyes. The grown-up takes some away.

Step 3 You open your eyes. Count how many are left.

Step 4 Tell how many are missing.

If you are right, you color a circle.
If you are wrong, the grown-up colors a circle.

Your circles: ◯ ◯ ◯ ◯ ◯ ◯

The grown-up's circles: ◯ ◯ ◯ ◯ ◯ ◯

Hilda Hid It

Hilda is a funny robot.

Hilda hides things.

How many beds are in your house? _____

Hilda hides 1.

How many beds now?

_____ – 1 = _____

How many chairs are in your kitchen? _____

Hilda hides 2.

How many chairs now?

_____ – 2 = _____

How many coats are in your house? _____

Hilda hides 3.

How many coats now?

_____ – 3 = _____

How many towels are in your bathroom? _____

Hilda hides 1.

How many now?

_____ – 1 = _____

Lose and Win Game

Play this game with a grown-up.

You need **20** pennies or paper clips.

You take 10 and your grown-up takes 10.

You also need something **VERY** small, like a **bean.**

Here is the game board.

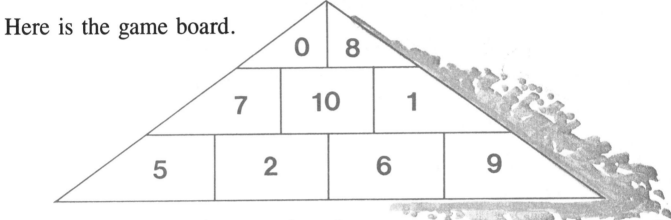

You toss a bean on the game board.

What number did you get? _____

Take away that many pennies from **your penny pile.**

How many pennies do you have left? _____

Your grown-up tosses a bean.

What number did your grown-up get? _____

Your grown-up takes away that many **pennies.**

How many pennies does your grown-up have left? _____

Who has more pennies now? _____ **Hooray, the winner!**

Play again. Who is the winner? _____

Subtracting from 10

Tic-Tac-Toe

Look at the boxes.

Put in the answers.

Color the **3** boxes with the same answer.

4 + 0	13 − 8	9 + 2
4		
7 − 3	6 + 4	10 + 1
	10	
10 − 2	3 + 5	13 − 5

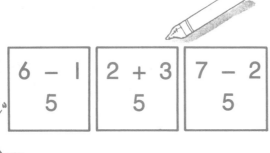

6 − 1	2 + 3	7 − 2
5	5	5

You found tic-tac-toe.

Play again.

12 − 8	2 + 4	5 + 4
8 + 2	15 − 9	7 + 2
7 + 5	13 − 7	6 + 6

Tic-Tac-Toe

Play these tic-tac-toe games with a grown-up.

Play them just like all tic-tac-toe games.

Before you mark **X** or **O**, you must add or subtract.

If your answer is right, put your mark in the box.

If your answer is wrong, try again.

When you get the right answer, put your mark in the box.

Take turns. Try to mark **3** boxes in a row.

8 – 5	6 + 6	3 + 8
6 + 7	8 – 3	13 – 3
3 + 2	9 + 1	5 + 8

8 + 9	6 – 2	12 – 3
8 + 4	8 + 8	7 – 3
12 – 4	8 – 4	8 + 10

10 – 3	11 – 3	6 + 4
11 – 4	10 + 5	15 – 5
13 + 2	10 – 4	13 – 3

Adding and Subtracting with Basic Facts: Sums to 15

Name _____

Add 10

Here is a game board.

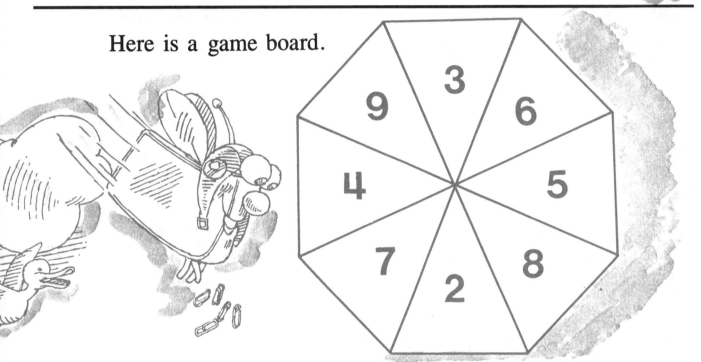

Drop a paper clip on the board.

What number did you get? _____

Add 10 to the number. _+10_

Write the sum. _____

Play again.

Write the number. _____

Add 10. _____

Write the sum. _____

What was your best score? _____

Play again.

Write the number. _____

Add 10. _+10_

Write the sum. _____

Play again.

Write the number. _____

Add 10. _____

Write the sum. _____

Rainbow Numbers

Play this game with a grown-up.

Toss a coin or a paper clip on the game board.
Add or subtract. Color the answer on your number rainbow.
The first person who colors in a rainbow wins the game.

Game Board

| 11-3 | 10+9 | 8+9 | 6+4 | 5+7 | 9+4 |
| 8+8 | 15-5 | 12-3 | 8+6 | 7+4 | 6+7 |

Your rainbow   **Your grown-up's rainbow**

Adding and Subtracting with Basic Facts: Sums to 19

Heads or Tails

LESSON 19

Toss a coin.

Heads = 10 points.

Tails = 5 points.

Play the game.

Heads   Tails

Toss 1 _____

Toss 2 _____

Toss 3 _____

Add _____

Ring the answer.

15 20 25 30

Play again.

Toss 1 _____

Toss 2 _____

Toss 3 _____

Add _____

Ring the answer.

15 20 25 30

Play again.

Toss 1 _____

Toss 2 _____

Toss 3 _____

Add _____

Ring the answer.

15 20 25 30

Play again.

Toss 1 _____

Toss 2 _____

Toss 3 _____

Add _____

Ring the answer.

15 20 25 30

Adding 5s and 10s: Three Addends

The 77 Game

Play this game with a grown-up.

Make number cards like these.

Pick a number card.   Your 77 board   Your grown-up's board

Write the number in
a square.

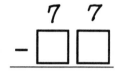   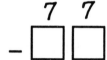

Pick another card.

Write the number in the other square.
Subtract.

Your grown-up does the same.

Who has the greater score?

_____

Hooray, the winner!

Play again with **88**.

Play again with **99**.

Subtracting 2-Digit Numbers

The Square Family

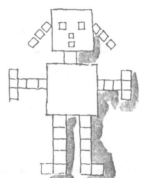

This is a square girl.	This is **not** a square girl.
Draw a square hat.	Draw a square house.
Draw a square dog.	Draw a square cat.

What Rolls?

Do this with a grown up.

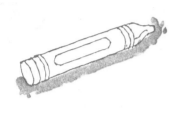

Can you roll a crayon?   Can you roll a shoe?

yes   no   yes   no

Which of these things can you roll? Find some and try it.

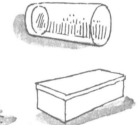

Draw things that roll.

Draw things that do not roll.

Can you roll yourself? _____

Identifying Attributes of Solid Figures

A Shape Hunt

Look for a square, a circle, and a rectangle in your house.

Find a square.
Where was it? Make a drawing.

Find a circle.
Where was it? Make a drawing.

Find a rectangle. Where was it? Make a drawing.

Shape Game

Play this game with a grown-up.

Get a marker for each player. You can use a coin.

Put the markers on START.

Make GAME CARDS like these.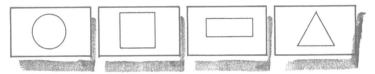

Turn the cards upside down. Mix them up.

Player I picks a card and moves his marker to that shape.

Replace the card. Mix up the cards again. Player **2** takes a turn. The first player to FINISH wins!

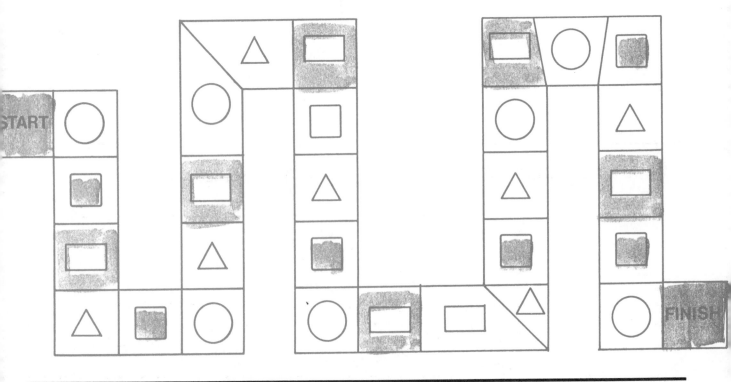

Identifying Squares, Rectangles, Circles and Triangles

A Pencil Long

Trace your pencil in the box.

Put your finger under the drawing.

Is your finger longer?   yes   no

Is your finger shorter?   yes   no

Is your finger as long as the pencil? yes   no

Find something as long as your pencil.

Draw it.

Find something longer than your pencil.

Draw it.

Find something shorter than your pencil.

Draw it.

A Trip Across Your Room

Do this with a grown-up.

Walk across the room.

How many steps did you take? _____

How many steps did the grown-up take? _____

Take baby steps across the room.

How many baby steps did you take? _____

How many baby steps did the grown-up take? _____

Take giant steps across the room.

How many giant steps did you take? _____

How many giant steps did the grown-up take? _____

Measure other things.

How far is it across the kitchen?

_____ steps _____ baby steps _____ giant steps

How far is your room from the kitchen?

_____ steps _____ baby steps _____ giant steps

Your Shoe

Trace your shoe here.

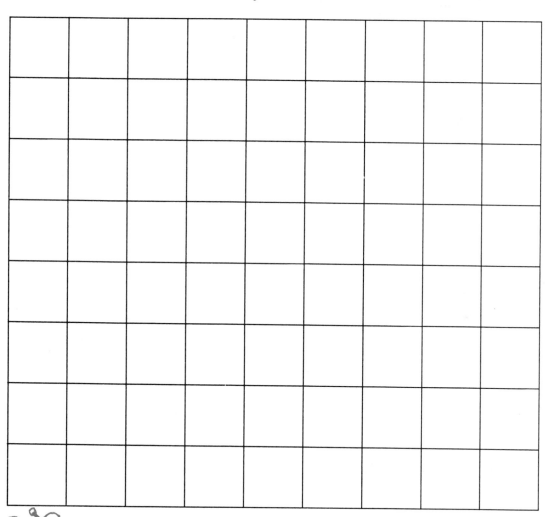

Color your drawing.

How many squares does your shoe touch? _____

Your Hand

Do this with a grown-up.

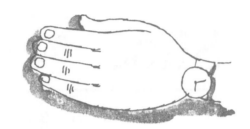

Trace your hand here.

Keep your fingers together.

Cover the drawing of your hand with little things.

Use dried beans, noodles, or coins.

What did you use to cover your hand? _____

How many did you use to cover your
hand? _____

Which is Heavier?

Hold a pencil in one hand.

Hold a cup in the other hand.

Which is heavier? Ring the answer.

Hold a book in one hand.

Hold 3 spoons in the other hand.

Which is heavier?

Hold 3 spoons in one hand.

Hold a glass in the other hand.

Which is heavier?

Hold a plate in one hand.

Hold 2 forks in the other hand.

Which is heavier?

Fill it Up

Do this with a grown-up.

Get a big bowl.

Get a cup.

Fill the cup with water.

Pour the water into the bowl.

Fill the cup again.

Pour the water into the bowl.

How many cups do you need to fill the bowl? _____

Ask your grown-up to try.

How many cups did your grown-up need? _____

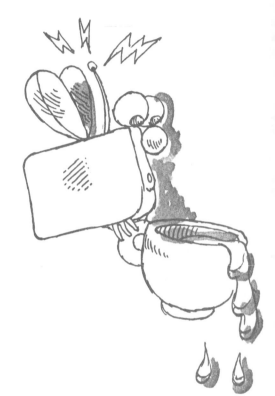

Try this with a pot.   Try this with a pan.

Use the cup to fill a pot. Use the cup to fill a pan.

How many cups did you need? _____

How many cups did you need? _____

Clocks

Look at a clock or a watch

Ring the kind you have.

Show the time you see.

   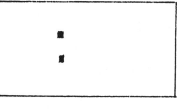

How many clocks and watches are in your house? _____

What do you like to eat in the morning? _____
Draw a picture.

What do you like to eat at night? _____
Draw a picture.

My Day

Do this with a grown-up.   Tell about your day.

I go to bed at _____ o'clock.

I wake up at _____ o'clock.

I eat breakfast at _____ o'clock.

I go to school at _____ o'clock.

I come home from school at _____ o'clock.

I eat dinner at _____ o'clock.

Ring your favorite time of day.

morning   afternoon   night

Ask a grown-up about her day.

My grown-up wakes up at _____ o'clock.

My grown-up eats breakfast at _____ o'clock.

My grown-up eats dinner at _____ o'clock.

My grown-up goes to bed at _____ o'clock.

Ring your grown-up's favorite time of day.

morning   afternoon   night

How Tall — How Long

LESSON
26

Use your centimeter ruler for this page.

How tall is the girl?

How tall is the boy?

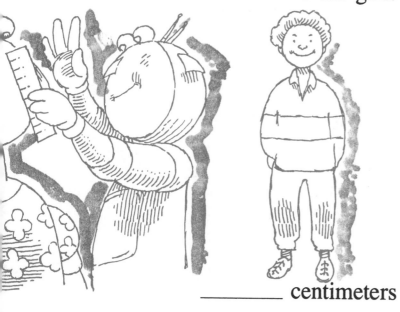

_____ centimeters

_____ centimeters

Who is taller?   girl   boy

How long is the pencil?

How long is the pen?

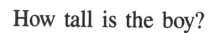

_____ centimeters

_____ centimeters

Which is longer?   pencil   pen

Guess How Long

Do this with a grown-up.
Use your centimeter ruler.
Look at the key. Guess how long it is?

Your guess: _____ centimeters

Your grown-up's guess: _____ centimeters

Measure and see. The key is _____ centimeters
long.

Look at the thumb. Guess how long it is?

Your guess: _____ centimeters

Your grown-up's guess: _____ centimeters

Measure and see. The thumb is _____
centimeters long.

Guess how long your thumb is?

Your guess: _____ centimeters

Your grown-up's guess: _____ centimeters

Measure and see. Your thumb is _____ centimeters long.

Using a Centimeter Ruler

Puzzle Parts

Part of the puzzle is missing.

Ring the missing part.

Part of the puzzle is missing.

Ring the missing part.

Numbers About Me

Do this with a grown-up.
You use numbers every day.
Fill in some special numbers that tell about you.

I am _____ years old.

My birthday is _____ .

My phone number is _____ .

My address is _____

_____ .

I have _____ stuffed animals.

My shoe size is _____ .

I can count up to _____ .

My lucky number is _____ .

My favorite TV show is on channel _____ .

Crazy Creatures

Here is a Fip.

Here are more Fips.

Here is a Boop.

Here are more Boops.

Are these Fips or Boops?   Fips   Boops

Are these Fips or Boops?   Fips   Boops

Draw a Fip.

Draw a Boop.

Your Kitchen

Do this with a grown-up.

Look around the kitchen.

Draw foods you drink.

Draw foods you chew.

Draw foods you like.

Draw a food you like and you chew.

Ask a grown-up to draw a food he likes and he chews.

Using Logical Thinking

Silly Pictures

Draw some silly pictures.

Draw a fat blue mouse with a red hat.

Draw a thin red mouse with a blue hat.

Draw a thin blue cat in a red hat playing with a fat red mouse.

Can You Find It?

Do this with a grown-up.

Try to find special things in your house.

Find something green and soft.

What is it? _____

Draw it.

Find something old and blue.

What is it? _____

Draw it.

Find something hard and red and new.

What is it? _____

Draw it.

Using Logical Thinking and Organizing Information

Number Pictures

Here is a **60** board.
Count by threes to **60**.
Start: 3, 6, 9, 12, 15.
Color these numbers
on the board.
Can you see a pattern?

1	2	3	4	5	6	7	8	9	10
11	12	13	14	15	16	17	18	19	20
21	22	23	24	25	26	27	28	29	30
31	32	33	34	35	36	37	38	39	40
41	42	43	44	45	46	47	48	49	50
51	52	53	54	55	56	57	58	59	60

Here is a **90** board.
Count by nines to **90**.
Start: 9, 18, 27, 36.
Color these numbers
on the board.
Can you see a pattern?

1	2	3	4	5	6	7	8	9	10
11	12	13	14	15	16	17	18	19	20
21	22	23	24	25	26	27	28	29	30
31	32	33	34	35	36	37	38	39	40
41	42	43	44	45	46	47	48	49	50
51	52	53	54	55	56	57	58	59	60
61	62	63	64	65	66	67	68	69	70
71	72	73	74	75	76	77	78	79	80
81	82	83	84	85	86	87	88	89	90

Pattern Page

Do this with a grown-up.

Here are two pattern drawings.
They have different patterns.

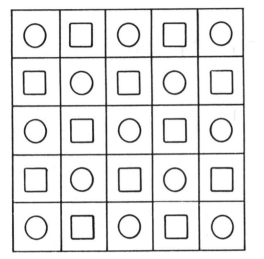 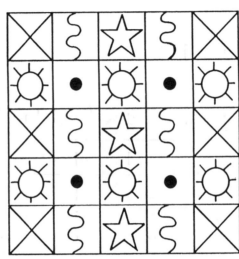

You can make a pattern drawing too.
Use colors or shapes in your drawing.
Ask a grown-up to make a drawing too.

My pattern drawing

My grown-up's pattern drawing

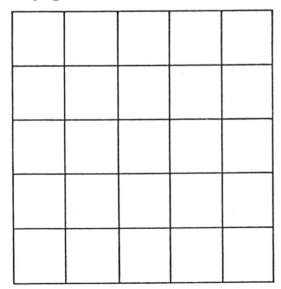

Making Patterns

Colored Boxes

Get a blue crayon 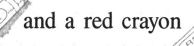 and a red crayon .

Here are 4 boxes. Color them.

RED	BLUE
BLUE	RED

Here are 4 more boxes. Color them.

RED	RED
RED	BLUE

Color these 4 boxes in a new way.

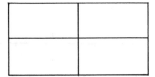

Here are more boxes. Color each set in a new way.

More Colored Boxes

Do this with a grown-up.

Get a blue crayon

Get a red crayon

Get a green crayon

Here are **3** boxes. Color them.

BLUE	RED	GREEN

Here are **3** more boxes. Color them.

BLUE	BLUE	GREEN

Color these **3** boxes in a new way.

Here are more boxes. Color each set in a new way.

Using Logical Thinking and Organizing Information

Practice your writing skills for numbers 1 thru 20.

Make up your own addition problems and solve.

Make up your own subtraction problems and solve.

Enrichment
Math Grade 2

AMERICAN
EDUCATION
PUBLISHING

Numbers Everywhere

Numbers are everywhere.
Numbers are in your house.
Small numbers. Big numbers.

Look in your living room for a number bigger than 10.

What number did you find?_____

Look in your bathroom for a number bigger than 20.

What number did you find?_____

Look in your kitchen for a number bigger than 50.

What number did you find?_____

Ring the bigger number.

    23 or 32   16 or 61   45 or 54

Family Matters

Do this with a grown-up.

Ask your grown-up to hop.
You count to **25**.
How many times did the grown-up hop?_____

You hop now.
Ask your grown-up to count.
How many times did you hop?_____

Count to **50**.
Ask your grown-up to tip-toe across the room.
Did your grown-up make it before **50**?_____

Ask your grown-up to count backwards from **30** to **5**.
You walk backwards across the room.
Did you make it before **5**?_____

House Points

Walk around your house getting points.

Count **2** points for each closet.
How many points for closets in your house?_____

Count **5** points for each table.
How many points for tables in your house?_____

Count **10** points for each mouth.
How many points for mouths in your house?_____

Count **5** points for each bed.
How many points for beds in your house?_____

Skip Counting by Twos, Fives, and Tens

Make A Number

Play this game with a grown-up.

Make number cards like these.

Turn the cards upside down.
Pick **2** cards and make a number.
With **5** and **9** you can make **59** or **95**.
Make the biggest number you can.
Take **3** turns.
The biggest number wins.

Who won?_____

My first number   My grown-up's first number

_____   _____

My second number   My grown-up's second number

_____   _____

My third number   My grown-up's third number

_____   _____

Catch the Sneak

All the numbers from **50** to **99** are here.

One sneaky number shows up two times.

Find the sneak by counting from **50** to **99**.

Cross out each number as you go.

When you are done, you will see the sneak.

66   92   53   85   50   96   75

84   73   63   89   83   86   65

9   91   98   93   78   54   87
          56
      64   79   71   97
                              60
      67   80   51   77   88   72

94   58   84   99
                62
81   70   74   82   95
          90
61   52   69   68
      57   76   55

What is the sneaky number? _____

Put Them in Order

Play this game with a grown-up.

Toss a coin on the board.
Write the number on your score card.
Write it in any of the **3** spaces.
You can erase an old number to write a new number.
The first player to get **3** numbers in order
like this, **25 41 62**, wins.

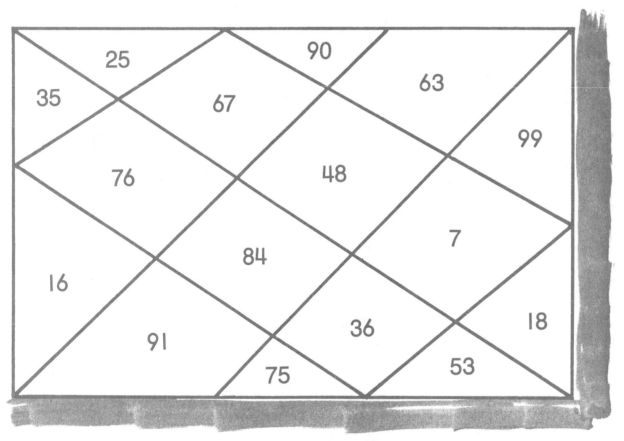

Your score card   Your grown-up's score card

100 Every Which Way

You need a blue crayon, a yellow crayon, and a red crayon.

Color 100 squares.

Color some yellow, some blue, some red.

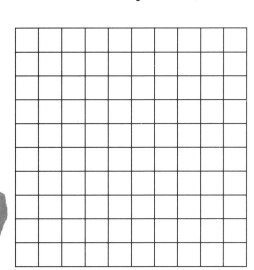

My drawing has ____ blue squares.

My drawing has ____ yellow squares.

My drawing has ____ red squares.

Color these 100 squares in a new way.

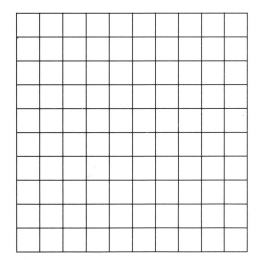

My drawing has ____ blue squares.

My drawing has ____ yellow squares.

My drawing has ____ red squares.

Number Contest

Have a contest with a grown-up.

Write the numbers from **75** to **100**.

You work on this page.

Your grown-up works on another sheet of paper.

See who can finish first.

When you are ready and set, then go.

Who finished first? _____

Get **2** new pieces of paper. Have another contest.

This time write the numbers from **20** to **80**.

Who finished first? _____

How Many?

Here are 100 circles.

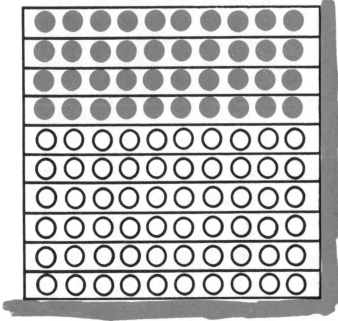

How many circles are in each row? _____

How many rows are in color? _____

How many circles are in color? _____

Here are 100 more circles.

How many circles are in each row? _____

How many rows are in color? _____

How many circles are in color? _____

So Many Circles

Play this game with a grown-up. You need a crayon and something small like a coin.

Toss the coin on the Gameboard.

Color that number of circles on your card.

Color the circles row by row.

Color all your circles first, and then you win.

Your Card

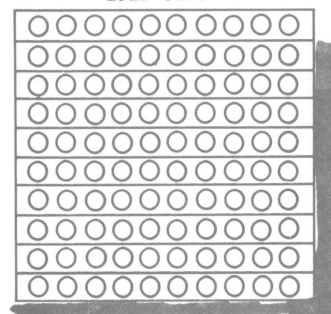

GAMEBOARD

5	3
1	9
7	4
0	2
6	8

Your Grown-Up's Card

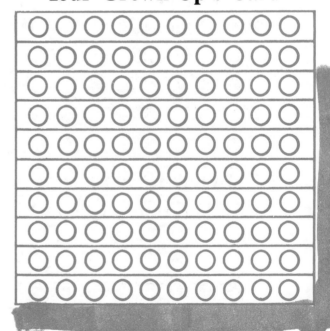

Count by 10

1	2	3	4	5	6	7	8	9	10
11	12	13	14	15	16	17	18	19	20
21	22	23	24	25	26	27	28	29	30
31	32	33	34	35	36	37	38	39	40
41	42	43	44	45	46	47	48	49	50
51	52	53	54	55	56	57	58	59	60
61	62	63	64	65	66	67	68	69	70
71	72	73	74	75	76	77	78	79	80
81	82	83	84	85	86	87	88	89	90
91	92	93	94	95	96	97	98	99	100

Start at 5.
Count 10 more.
Where are you now?

_____

Count 10 more.
Where are you now?

_____

Count 10 more.
Where are you now?

_____

Start at **22**.
Count 10 more.
Where are you now?

_____

Count 10 more.
Where are you now?

_____

Count 10 more.
Where are you now?

_____

Looking for Patterns in a 100-chart

Odd and Even

Do this with a grown-up.
You need a crayon and **30** little things like
uncooked noodles.

Take **1** noodle. Can two people share it equally?
No. So, **1** is an **ODD** number.

Take **2** noodles. Can two people share them equally?
Yes. So, **2** is an **EVEN** number.

Use noodles to test the numbers up to **30**.
Color even numbers red.
Color odd numbers blue.

1	2	3	4	5	6	7	8	9	10
11	12	13	14	15	16	17	18	19	20
21	22	23	24	25	26	27	28	29	30

Identifying Odd and Even Numbers

Pennies and Dimes

How much money is this? _____

How much money is this? _____

Make **52¢** in a new way. Use only pennies and dimes.

How many pennies did you use? _____

How many dimes? _____

Make **52¢** in a new way. Use only pennies and dimes.

How many pennies did you use? _____

How many dimes? _____

Money Mats

You and your grown-up take turns picking money bubbles.
How much is your bubble worth?
Color a box worth the same amount on your money mat.
The first player to color **3** boxes in a row wins.

Your money mat

23¢	45¢	23¢	73¢
65¢	73¢	65¢	45¢
45¢	73¢	73¢	23¢
45¢	65¢	65¢	23¢

Your grown-up's money mat

45¢	65¢	73¢	23¢
23¢	65¢	65¢	45¢
73¢	45¢	23¢	73¢
23¢	73¢	65¢	45¢

Money Bubbles

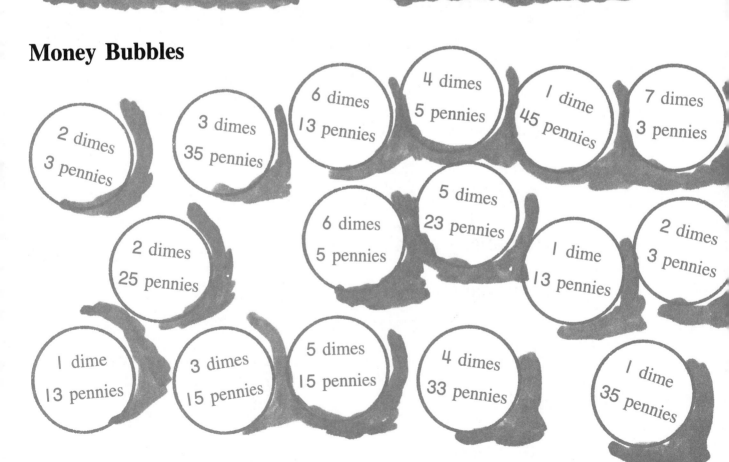

2 dimes 3 pennies

3 dimes 35 pennies

6 dimes 13 pennies

4 dimes 5 pennies

1 dime 45 pennies

7 dimes 3 pennies

2 dimes 25 pennies

6 dimes 5 pennies

5 dimes 23 pennies

1 dime 13 pennies

2 dimes 3 pennies

1 dime 13 pennies

3 dimes 15 pennies

5 dimes 15 pennies

4 dimes 33 pennies

1 dime 35 pennies

Using Money to Rename Tens and Ones

Ring It

Draw rings on the pegs to get points. Someone got **214** points here.

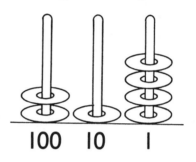

100   10   1

1. Draw rings to get **111** points.

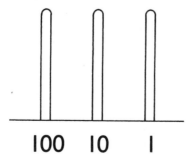

100   10   1

2. Draw rings to get **211** points.

100   10   1

3. Draw rings to get **74** points.

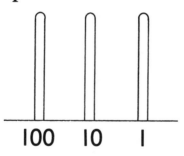

100   10   1

4. Draw rings to get **999** points.

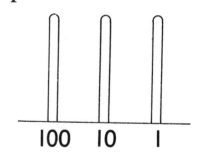

100   10   1

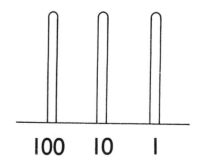

Exploring Place Value in 3-Digit Numbers

Hit the Number

Play this game with a grown-up.
You need **6** small things like beans.

Use a sheet of paper to draw a target like this.

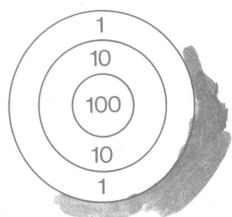

Drop all **6** beans on the target.
When all **6** beans are in place, write your score.
Play **2** times.

My first try

_____ _____ _____
hundreds   tens   ones

My second try

_____ _____ _____
hundreds   tens   ones

My grown-up's first try

_____ _____ _____
hundreds   tens   ones

My grown-up's second try

_____ _____ _____
hundreds   tens   ones

Using Place Value to Write 3-Digit Numbers

LESSON
9

Toss and Add

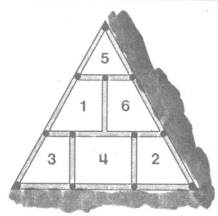

Here is a number board.
Toss two coins or beans on the board.
Add the numbers you get.
Play **8** rounds.

Round 1
_____
+ _____
_____

Round 2
_____
+ _____
_____

Round 3
_____
+ _____
_____

Round 4
_____
+ _____
_____

Round 5
_____
+ _____
_____

Round 6
_____
+ _____
_____

Round 7
_____
+ _____
_____

Round 8
_____
+ _____
_____

What was your best score? _____

What is the best possible score in the game? _____

Tic-Tac-Toe

Play these tic-tac-toe games with a grown-up.

Play just like all tic-tac-toe games.

Before you mark **X** or **O**, you must add or subtract.

If your answer is right, put your mark in the box.

If your answer is wrong, try again.

When you get the right answer, put your mark in the box.

12 − 5	6 + 3	10 − 3
11 − 3	8 + 4	9 + 3
9 − 5	5 + 7	8 + 3

9 − 4	12 − 8	9 − 5
8 + 4	11 − 6	7 + 5
12 − 4	6 − 4	7 + 3

8 + 2	3 + 9	12 + 4
8 − 3	7 + 5	9 − 6
12 − 7	4 + 6	11 − 3

11 − 4	12 − 6	9 + 3
7 + 3	11 − 8	11 − 2
11 − 5	8 + 4	7 − 5

Adding and Subtracting with Basic Facts: Sums to 12

On or Off The Plate

You need a plate and 12 little things like beans.

Throw **8** beans and try to get them on the plate.

How many are on the plate? _____

How many are off the plate? _____

$$\underline{\hspace{2cm}}_{\text{on}} + \underline{\hspace{2cm}}_{\text{off}} = 8$$

$$\underline{\hspace{2cm}}_{\text{off}} + \underline{\hspace{2cm}}_{\text{on}} = 8$$

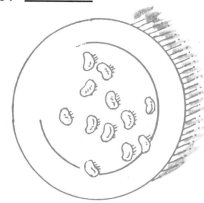

Throw 10 beans.

How many are on the plate? _____

How many are off the plate? _____

$$\underline{\hspace{2cm}}_{\text{on}} + \underline{\hspace{2cm}}_{\text{off}} = 10$$

$$\underline{\hspace{2cm}}_{\text{off}} + \underline{\hspace{2cm}}_{\text{on}} = 10$$

Throw 12 beans.

How many are on the plate? _____

How many are off the plate? _____

$$\underline{\hspace{2cm}}_{\text{on}} + \underline{\hspace{2cm}}_{\text{off}} = 12$$

$$\underline{\hspace{2cm}}_{\text{off}} + \underline{\hspace{2cm}}_{\text{on}} = 12$$

4 in a Row

Play this game with a grown-up.

Make **8** number cards like these.

Turn the cards upside down.

Pick a card. Both players match the number on the
card with an answer on their playing boards.

Color that box.

You can color only one box each time.

Keep playing until someone gets 4 boxes in a row.

Your Game Board

15 − 7	6 +6	9 +2	12 − 3
8 +6	6 +7	14 − 6	8 +2
9 +5	7 +3	9 +4	8 +4
8 +6	9 +6	11 − 2	8 +7

Your Grown-up's Game Board

13 − 5	7 +7	15 − 6	5 +5
9 +3	12 − 4	6 +4	8 +3
7 +4	14 − 5	11 − 3	8 +5
13 − 4	9 +6	7 +5	8 +7

Adding and Subtracting with Basic Facts: Sums to 15

Look for Cover

Draw **7** circles.

Cover up **2** circles. How many are left? _____

Cover up **5** circles. How many are left? _____

Draw **12** circles.

Cover up **3** circles. How many are left? _____

Cover up **9** circles. How many are left? _____

Draw **15** circles.

Cover up **8** circles. How many are left? _____

Cover up **7** circles. How many are left? _____

Math Baseball

You need 4 little things like coins.

You are the batter. Your grown-up is the pitcher.

Each pitch is a math question. Each answer is a hit.

Ask for the pitch you want: a single, a double, a triple, or a home run.

Give the right answer and you get a hit.

Give the wrong answer and you're out.

3 outs end the game.

Get 5 players home before the game ends and you win.

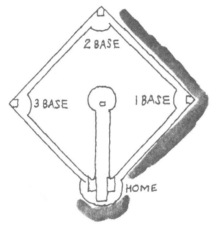

How many players did you get home? _____

Single Questions		
3 + 2	10 − 2	6 + 4
8 − 3	9 − 2	6 − 6

Double Questions		
8 + 8	12 − 3	15 − 4
9 + 5	11 − 4	7 + 5

Triple Questions		
16 − 8	8 + 6	12 − 5
7 + 8	14 − 7	14 − 6

Home Run Questions		
15 − 8	15 − 7	17 − 9
16 − 7	14 − 8	13 − 5

Adding and Subtracting with Basic Facts: Sums to 18

Mistakes All Over

Ray is a broken robot.
Some of Ray's answers are correct.
Some of Ray's answers are mistakes.
Mark the paper.
Put a ✔ on the correct answers.
Put a **X** on the mistakes.

$$\begin{array}{r} 3 \\ +8 \\ \hline 12 \end{array} \qquad \begin{array}{r} 7 \\ +7 \\ \hline 18 \end{array} \qquad \begin{array}{r} 9 \\ -5 \\ \hline 4 \end{array} \qquad \begin{array}{r} 6 \\ +7 \\ \hline 13 \end{array}$$

$$\begin{array}{r} 12 \\ -8 \\ \hline 6 \end{array} \qquad \begin{array}{r} 18 \\ -9 \\ \hline 7 \end{array} \qquad \begin{array}{r} 13 \\ -7 \\ \hline 7 \end{array} \qquad \begin{array}{r} 9 \\ +7 \\ \hline 16 \end{array}$$

How many correct answers did you find? _____
How many mistakes did you find? _____

Fill in Your Circle

Play this game with a grown-up.
You need something little like a paper clip.

Toss a paper clip on the GAMEBOARD.
When it lands, add or subtract.
Color the answer in your NUMBER CIRCLE.
Finish coloring your NUMBER CIRCLE first, and
you win the game.

GAMEBOARD

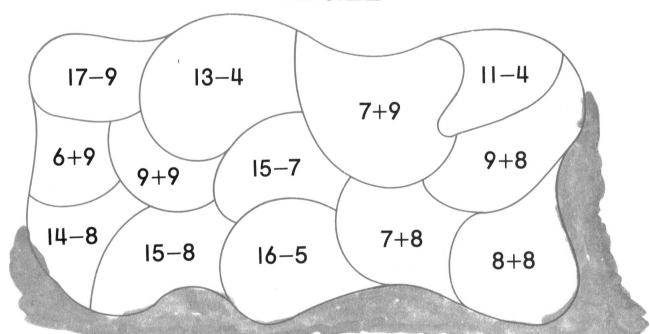

YOUR CIRCLE

YOUR GROWN-UP'S CIRCLE

Adding and Subtracting with Basic Facts: Sums to 18

Find the Oddball and More

Add and subtract.

Color the box with a different answer.

14 – 8	13 – 6
5 + 1	11 – 5

Try again.

16 – 7	18 – 9
12 – 5	6 + 3

How many letters in TOOTH? _____

How many letters in BRUSH? _____

How many letters in TOOTHBRUSH? _____

How many letters in PLAY? _____

How many letters in GROUND? _____

How many letters in PLAYGROUND? _____

Little Checkers

Play this game with a grown-up.
You need something small for checkers like bits of colored paper.

Play like regular checkers, but with one difference.
Solve the math problem before moving to a new square.

	12−4		6+8		9−3		13−5
8+3		7−5		11−5		7+7	
	17−9		7+6		13−5		8+4
18−9		14−6		8+5		12−6	
	9+4		8+3		16−8		6+7
13−7		7+5		12−4		15−8	
	17−8		9+7		14−7		9+6

Who won the game? _____

Adding and Subtracting with Basic Facts: Sums to 18

Make 10 Any Way You Can

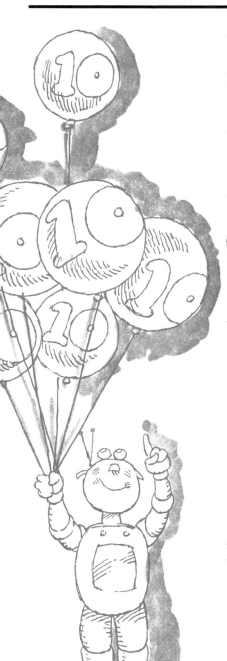

Use the numbers 1, 2, 3, 4, 5, 6, 7, 8, and 9 to make 10.

You can add. Here is one way.

$$3 + 1 + 3 + 2 + 1 = 10$$

You can add and subtract. Here is one way.

$$8 + 4 + 3 - 5 = 10$$

Try to find 10 ways to make 10.

Try to find more ways.

Write down every way you find.

How many ways did you find? _____

Math Star

Play this game with a grown-up.

Are you a math star?

Answer the problems.

If you get a problem right, color a star.

If you get a problem wrong, your grown-up colors a star.

Who has the most stars? _____

You are the winner!

$$\begin{array}{r} 26 \\ + 11 \\ \hline \end{array} \qquad \begin{array}{r} 22 \\ + 13 \\ \hline \end{array} \qquad \begin{array}{r} 42 \\ + 25 \\ \hline \end{array} \qquad \begin{array}{r} 18 \\ + 81 \\ \hline \end{array}$$

$$\begin{array}{r} 57 \\ + 32 \\ \hline \end{array} \qquad \begin{array}{r} 34 \\ + 21 \\ \hline \end{array} \qquad \begin{array}{r} 44 \\ - 11 \\ \hline \end{array} \qquad \begin{array}{r} 56 \\ - 34 \\ \hline \end{array}$$

$$\begin{array}{r} 78 \\ - 22 \\ \hline \end{array} \qquad \begin{array}{r} 48 \\ - 22 \\ \hline \end{array} \qquad \begin{array}{r} 27 \\ - 15 \\ \hline \end{array} \qquad \begin{array}{r} 99 \\ - 33 \\ \hline \end{array}$$

Your stars

Your grown-up's stars

Adding and Subtracting 2-Digit Numbers Without Renaming

LESSON
15

Amazing 9

Begin with **5**

Add **9**. What do you get? _____

Add **9** again. What do you get? _____

Add **9** again. What do you get? _____

Add **9** again. What do you get? _____

Do you see a pattern? _____

Begin with **8**.

Add **9**. What do you get? _____

Add **9** again. What do you get? _____

Add **9** again. What do you get? _____

Add **9** again. What do you get? _____

Do you see a pattern? _____

Begin with **9**

Add **9**. What do you get? _____

Add **9** again. What do you get? _____

Add **9** again. What do you get? _____

Add **9** again. What do you get? _____

Do you see a pattern? _____

Adding 1- and 2-Digit Numbers to Discover a Pattern

Family Ages

Do this with a grown-up.

How old are you? _____
What year were you born? _____
How old will you be in 5 years? _____
How old will you be in 10 years? _____
How old will you be in 20 years? _____
How old were you 2 years ago? _____
How old were you 5 years ago? _____

How old is your grown-up? _____
What year was your grown-up born? _____
How old will your grown-up be in 5 years? _____
How old will your grown-up be in 10 years? _____
How old will your grown-up be in 20 years? _____
How old was your grown-up 2 years ago? _____
How old was your grown-up 5 years ago? _____
How old was your grown-up 10 years ago? _____
How old was your grown-up when you were born? _____
Your grown-up is older than you. How much older? _____

Adding and Subtracting 1- and 2-Digit Numbers

Darts

Here is Harry's dart board.

How many points did Harry get? _____

Here is your dart board.
Drop 4 coins or beans on the board.

How many points did you get? _____
Start with **99**. Subtract your score.
Start with **99**. Subtract Harry's score.
Who won, you or Harry? _____

$$\begin{array}{r} 99 \\ - \\ \hline \end{array}$$ your score

$$\begin{array}{r} 99 \\ - \\ \hline \end{array}$$ Harry's score

---

Adding and Subtracting 2-Digit Numbers   **107**

A Giant Number Story

Do this with a grown-up.

Fill in the blanks with numbers.

Last week a family of giants came to town.

There were ____ girl giants and ____ boy giants.

How many giants in all? ____

The giants met a boy named Jack.

Jack said, "Come to my house."

Jack gave the giants beans for dinner.

He gave them ____ lima beans.

He gave them ____ green beans.

How many beans in all? ____

Jane Giant planted beans in the garden.

The next morning she saw a giant bean stalk.

She climbed up.

When Jane got to the top she saw magic plants.

She saw ____ gold plants and ____ silver plants.

How many plants in all? ____

Eating magic plants makes you bigger.

Jane gave the plants to Jack.

Jack ate a gold plant.

He grew ____ feet, and then he grew ____ feet.

How many feet did Jack grow? ____

Now Jack was a giant too. "Hooray," said Jack.

"I love being a giant."

Would you like to be a giant? ____

Calendar Math

Sunday	Monday	Tuesday	Wednesday	Thursday	Friday	Saturday
					1	2
3	4	5	6	7	8	9
10	11	12	13	14	15	16
17	18	19	20	21	22	23
24	25	26	27	28	29	30

Find the dates.

Example
The 1st Friday ___1___
The 2nd Friday ___8___
Add ___9___

Subtract Up and Down

The 4th Sunday ____   The 4th Thursday ____

The 3rd Sunday ____   The 3rd Thursday ____

    Subtract ____   Subtract ____

Add First and Last

The 1st day of the month ____   The 2nd day of the month ____

The last day of the month ____   The 2nd to last day of the month ____

    Add ____   Add ____

Add Crisscross

The 1st Sunday ____   The 1st Monday ____

The 2nd Monday ____   The 2nd Sunday ____

    Add ____   Add ____

Adding and Subtracting 2-Digit Numbers with Renaming

Rainbow Colors

Play this game with a grown-up.

Take turns picking **2** numbers and adding.

After you add, color in the right part of your rainbow.

If that part is already colored, you miss a turn.

You win if you color your rainbow first.

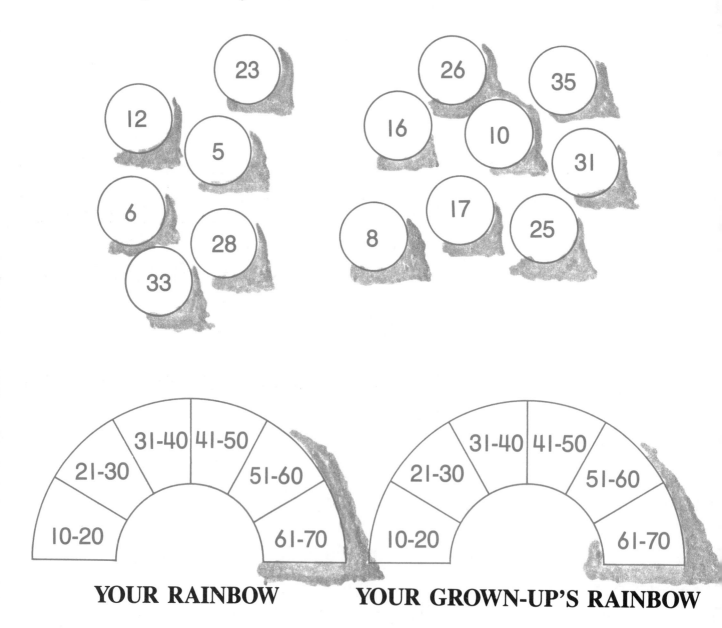

YOUR RAINBOW   **YOUR GROWN-UP'S RAINBOW**

Words Are Worth It

Letters are worth points.

3 points **A B C D**	4 points **E F G H**	5 points **I J K L**
7 points **M N O P**	8 points **Q R S T U**	9 points **V W X Y Z**

Words are worth points.

ME is worth 11 points. 7 points for **M** plus 4 points for **E**.

How many points for **CAT**? _____
How many points for **TV**? _____

How many points for your name? _____
Write a friend's name. _____
How many points for a friend's name? _____

Box Numbers

Play this game with a grown-up.

You need a coin or paper clip.

Use a sheet of paper to make a gameboard like this.

638	378	259
177	586	465

Drop a coin on the board.

Write the number you get on your score card.

Subtract. The biggest answer wins.

SCORE CARD

Your round 1

744

−____

_____

Your grown-up's round 1

744

−____

_____

Your round 2

832

−____

_____

Your grown-up's round 2

832

−____

_____

Your round 3

891

−____

_____

Your grown-up's round 3

891

−____

_____

Subtracting 3-Digit Numbers with Renaming

Adding and Subtracting Around the House

LESSON
19

Start with **456**.

Look at a calendar. Pick a number. _____

Subtract the number.   456

                               – ____

                               _____

Start with **876**.

Look at a newspaper. Pick a number. _____

Subtract.   876

                               – ____

                               _____

Start with **200**.

Look at a book. Pick a page number. _____

Add.   200

                               + ____

                               _____

Write your telephone number. __ __ __ __ __ __ __

Add all the numbers. What is the sum? _____

Pick a Number

Play this game with a grown-up.
Make **6** number cards like this.

Turn the cards upside down.

Pick **3** cards.

Use the numbers to fill in blanks on your number board.

Play **3** rounds.

Your Round 1 Board 244 + _____ _____	**Your Grown-Up's Round 1 Board** 244 + _____ _____
Your Round 2 Board 389 + _____ _____	**Your Grown-Up's Round 2 Board** 389 + _____ _____
Your Round 3 Board 269 + _____ _____	**Your Grown-Up's Round 3 Board** 269 + _____ _____

Adding 3-Digit Numbers with Renaming

How Long?

Get **2** spoons.
Lay them end to end.
Put a pencil next to the spoons.

Ring the answer.

The pencil is   LONGER   SHORTER   THE SAME

Put your foot next to the spoons.

Your foot is   LONGER   SHORTER   THE SAME

Put a toy next to the spoons.

Your toy is   LONGER   SHORTER   THE SAME

Put your toothbrush next to the spoons.

Your toothbrush is   LONGER   SHORTER   THE SAME

Look for something THE SAME as the spoons.

What did you find? _____

Foot Time

Trace your foot on a piece of paper. Cut it out.

Trace your grown-up's foot on another piece of paper. Cut it out.

Search your house.

Find something about the same size as your foot.

What is it? _____

Draw a picture.

Find something about the same size as your grown-up's foot.

What is it? _____

Draw a picture.

Find something longer than your foot and shorter than your
grown-up's foot. What is it? _____

Ask your grown-up to draw a picture.

Measuring Length

Inches and Centimeters

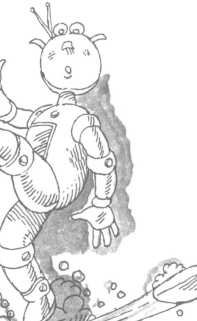

Use your inch ruler and your centimeter ruler.
Ring the right answer.

Measure a bar of soap.

The soap is	The soap is
longer than **3** inches	longer than **10** centimeters
shorter than **3** inches	shorter than **10** centimeters
just **3** inches	just **10** centimeters

Measure a door key.

The key is	The key is
longer than **2** inches	longer than **7** centimeters
shorter than **2** inches	shorter than **7** centimeters
just **2** inches	just **7** centimeters

Measure a salt shaker.

The shaker is	The shaker is
longer than **4** inches	longer than **12** centimeters
shorter than **4** inches	shorter than **12** centimeters
just **4** inches	just **12** centimeters

The Size of You

Ask a grown-up to help you measure.

Measure your thumb.
Your thumb is nearest to ____ inches.
Your thumb is nearest to ____ centimeters.

Measure your big toe.
Your big toe is nearest to ____ inches.
Your big toe is nearest to ____ centimeters.

Measure your nose.
Your nose is nearest to ____ inches.
Your nose is nearest to ____ centimeters.

Measure your grown-up's thumb.
Your grown-up's thumb is nearest to ____ inches.
Your grown-up's thumb is nearest to ____ centimeters.

Measure your grown-up's nose.
Your grown-up's nose is nearest to ____ inches.
Your grown-up's nose is nearest to ____ centimeters.

Using Rulers to Measure Inches and Centimeters

Going Around

You need lots of little things like paper clips.

Get an envelope.
Put the paper clips all around the envelope.

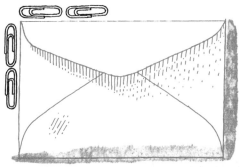

How many paper clips did you need? _____

Get a bar of soap.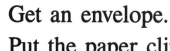
Put the paper clips all around the soap.
How many paper clips did you need? _____

How many babysteps does it take to
walk **across** your room? _____

How many babysteps does it take to
walk **around** your room? _____

Finding Perimeter with Non-standard Units

The Weight of Things

Do this with a grown-up
Get a can of food.
Look for the weight.
How much does it weigh? _____ oz or _____ grams

Hold the can in one hand.
Hold a bowl in your other hand.
Which is heavier? _____

Let your grown-up try.
Does your grown-up agree? _____

Get a jar of food.
Look for the weight.
How much does it weigh? _____ oz or _____ grams

Hold the jar in one hand.
Hold a plate in your other hand.
Which is heavier? _____

Let your grown-up try.
Does your grown-up agree? _____

Measuring Weights

Estimate It!

Look at a spoon.

Look at a cup.

How many spoons of water would it take to fill the cup?

DON'T DO IT! ESTIMATE IT!

What's your estimate? _____

Look at a cup.

Look at your bathtub.

How many cups of water would it take to fill the bathtub?

DON'T DO IT! ESTIMATE IT!

What's your estimate? _____

Look at a spoon.

Look at your bathtub.

How many spoons of water would it take to fill the bathtub?

DON'T DO IT! ESTIMATE IT!

What's your estimate? _____

Which Holds More?

Do this with a grown-up.
You need a cup, a bowl, and a pot.

  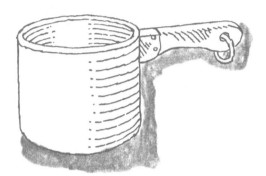

Fill the cup with water.
Pour the water into the bowl.
Fill the cup again.
Pour the water into the bowl again.
How many cups do you need to fill the bowl? _____

Fill the cup with water.
Pour the water into the pot.
Fill the cup again.
Pour the water into the pot again.
How many cups do you need to fill the pot? _____

Which holds more, the pot or the bowl? _____

Measuring Capacity

Dot to Dot

Draw from dot to dot. See what you get.

   Draw a line from 1 to **3**.

   Draw a line from **3** to 5.

   Draw a line from 5 to 2.

   Draw a line from 2 to 4.

   Draw a line from 4 to 1.

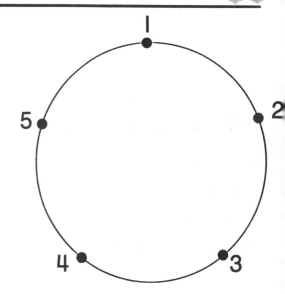

Did you draw a star? _____

Look for triangles.

How many do you see? _____

Color the triangles red.

Draw from dot to dot. See what you get.

   Draw a line from 1 to 4.

   Draw a line from 4 to 7.

   Draw a line from 7 to 2.

   Draw a line from 2 to 5.

   Draw a line from 5 to 8.

   Draw a line from 8 to 3.

   Draw a line from 3 to 6.

   Draw a line from 6 to 1.

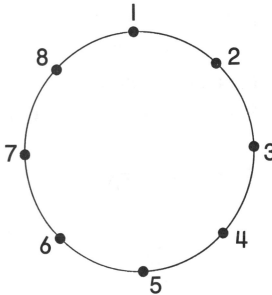

Did you draw another star? _____

Look for triangles.

How many do you see? _____

Color the triangles red.

Hidden Shapes

Do this with a grown-up.

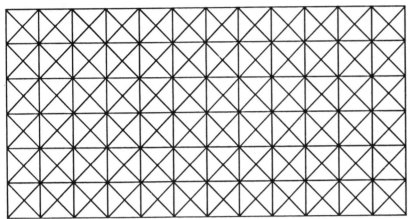

Look for **2** triangles.
Some are big. Some are little.
Color them blue.

Look for **2** rectangles.
Some are big. Some are little.
Color them yellow.

Look for **2** squares.
Some are big. Some are little.
Color them purple.

Look for hexagons.
Color I green.

Can you find other shapes?
Color them.

Identifying Geometric Shapes

Solid Shapes

This is a cylinder.
You can find cylinders in your house.

Can you find **3** different cylinders in your house?
What did you find?

_____

_____

_____

This is a rectangular prism.
You can find rectangular prisms in your house.

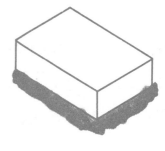

Can you find **3** different rectangular prisms in your house?
What did you find?

_____

_____

_____

Buildings

Do this with a grown-up.

You need **2** cylinders, like cans of food, or rolls of tissue.

You need **2** rectangular prisms, like cereal boxes, or tissue boxes.

Try to make this building.

Is your building sturdy?

     YES   NO

Try to make this building.

Is your building sturdy?

     YES   NO

Try to make this building.

Is your building sturdy?

     YES   NO

Make your own building.

Draw a picture of it.

Investigating Attributes of Solid Forms

The Time of Day

What time did you wake up this morning? _____
Fill in the clocks.

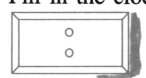 

What time did you go to school? _____
Fill in the clocks.

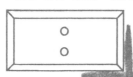 

What time is your bedtime? _____
Fill in the clocks.

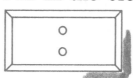

What time is dinner time? _____
Fill in the clocks.

What time is it now? _____
Fill in the clocks.

Time It

Do this with a grown-up.
You need a clock or a watch with a second hand.
Have your grown-up time you.

Can you hop for 1 minute?
Did you do it? _____

Can you hold your breath for 10 seconds?
Did you do it? _____

Can you sit and do nothing for **2** minutes?
(No laughing, no talking, no moving, no playing)
Did you do it? _____

Can you write your name 10 times in 1 minute?
Did you do it? _____

How long does it take you to clear the dinner table?
How long did it take you? _____

HONK

Investigating Elapsed Time

Can You See It?

Here is a robot, but only part of a robot.

Can you see it? _____

Look at this. What can it be? _____

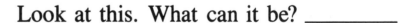

Look at this. What can it be? _____

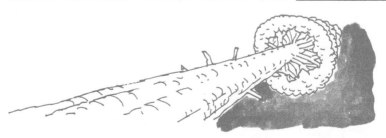

Look at this. What can it be? _____

Making Squares

Play this game with a grown-up.

Put your pencil on any dot.

Draw lines from one dot to another.

You can draw up, down, or across.

Do not lift your pencil.

Do not redraw any lines.

Try to make squares.

Keep going until you get stuck.

Here is a sample game.

Beginning of the game	**Middle of the game**	**End of the game**

Here are **2** boards for you.

Here are **2** boards for a grown-up.

Who got the most squares? _____

Using Spatial Thinking

Who Is Who?

Here are 4 rabbits.

Hoppy has the longest ears.

Jumpy is the smallest.

Skippy is between Hoppy and Jumpy.

Flippy plants the carrots.

Who is who? Write the names.

_____ _____ _____ _____

Here are 4 clowns.

Silly is the biggest.

Nutty is standing between Silly and Looney.

Foo Foo likes cookies.

Who is who? Write the names.

_____ _____ _____ _____

Estimate First

Do this with a grown-up.

How many spoons are in your kitchen drawer?
Make an estimate. _____
What does your grown-up estimate? _____
Count all the spoons.
How many did you count? _____

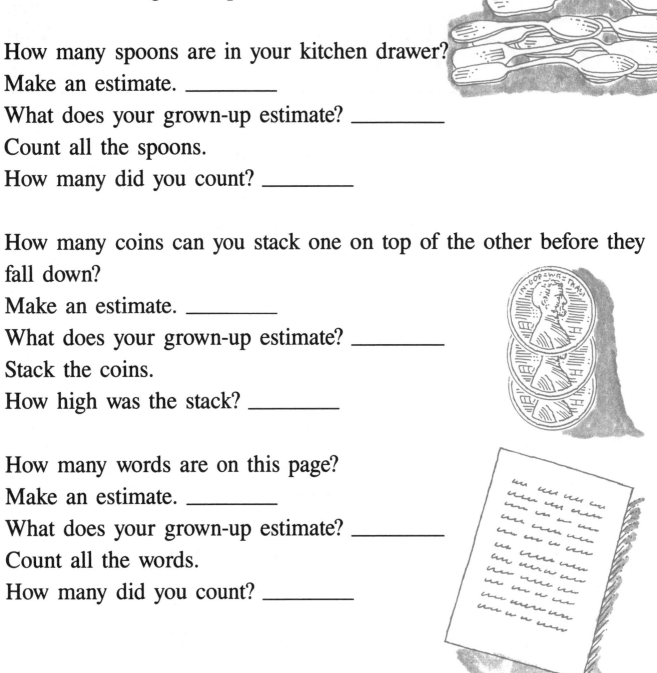

How many coins can you stack one on top of the other before they fall down?
Make an estimate. _____
What does your grown-up estimate? _____
Stack the coins.
How high was the stack? _____

How many words are on this page?
Make an estimate. _____
What does your grown-up estimate? _____
Count all the words.
How many did you count? _____

Fits the Bill

Find something bigger than a shoe
but smaller than a television.

What is it? _____

Find something bigger than a telephone
but smaller than a table.

What is it? _____

Find something bigger than a penny
but smaller than a toothbrush.

What is it? _____

Make your own bigger and smaller.

_____ is bigger than _____
but smaller than _____ .

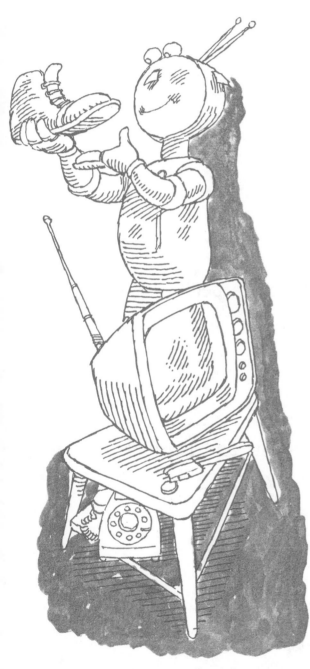

And And And

Do this with a grown-up.

Look in your house.

Find something blue. What is it? _____

Find something blue and old. (It could be the same as before.)

What is it? _____

Find something blue and old and you wear it.

What is it? _____

Think of all your friends and relatives.

Who is a boy? _____

Who is a boy and younger than you? _____

Who is a boy and is younger than you and has a pet? _____

Think of all your friends and relatives.

Who likes sports? _____

Who likes sports and comics? _____

Who likes sports and likes comics and is a girl? _____

Who likes sports and likes comics and is a girl and is older
than you? _____

Categorizing and Organizing Information

Hundreds of Patterns

Use the 100 board to add and subtract.
Color each answer on the board.
You will make a picture.

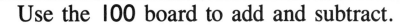

1	2	3	4	5	6	7	8	9	10
11	12	13	14	15	16	17	18	19	20
21	22	23	24	25	26	27	28	29	30
31	32	33	34	35	36	37	38	39	40
41	42	43	44	45	46	47	48	49	50
51	52	53	54	55	56	57	58	59	60
61	62	63	64	65	66	67	68	69	70
71	72	73	74	75	76	77	78	79	80
81	82	83	84	85	86	87	88	89	90
91	92	93	94	95	96	97	98	99	100

Start with 6.

Add 9 _____	Subtract 9 _____	Add 10 _____
Add 9 _____	Subtract 9 _____	Add 10 _____
Add 9 _____	Subtract 11 _____	Add 10 _____
Add 11 _____	Subtract 11 _____	Add 10 _____
Add 11 _____	Subtract 11 _____	Add 10 _____
Add 11 _____	Add 10 _____	Add 10 _____
Subtract 9 ____	Add 10 _____	Add 10 _____

Get 102

Do this with a grown-up.

Here is a **50** board. If you add the right way and follow the pattern, you will always get **102**. See if you can figure it out.

1	⭐2	3	4	5	6	7	8	⭐9	10
11	(12)	✓13	14	15	16	17	✓18	(19)	20
21	22	23	24	25	26	27	28	29	30
31	(32)	✓33	34	35	36	37	✓38	(39)	40
41	⭐42	43	44	45	46	47	48	⭐49	50

Add the **4** shaded numbers. What do you get? _____

Add the **4** circled numbers. What do you get? _____

Add the **4** numbers with stars. What do you get? _____

Add the **4** numbers with checks. What do you get? _____

Look for your own **102**. Color the numbers you add red.

Space Creatures

This is a visitor from the plant Gooney.
He has **2** heads 😊.
He has **3** eyes 👁 on each head 😊.
He has **1** nose ⌣ on each head 😊.
He has **2** mouths ⌣ on each head 😊.
He has **4** arms .
He has **3** legs .

Draw a family of **5** Gooneys.

How many heads are in the family? _____

How many mouths are in the famly? _____

How many eyes are in the family? _____

How many arms are in the family? _____

How many noses are in the family? _____

How many legs are in the family? _____

I know a Gooney family with

12 eyes

4 noses

4 heads

8 mouths

8 arms

6 legs

How many Gooneys are in this family? _____

What To Wear?

Do this with a grown-up.
In Kate's closet there are **3** shirts.

A red shirt
A blue shirt
A yellow shirt

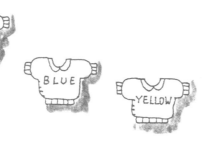

In Kate's closet there are **3** skirts.
A red skirt
A blue skirt
A yellow skirt

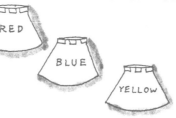

Kate can make lots of outfits. Color these **9** outfits so that each one is different.

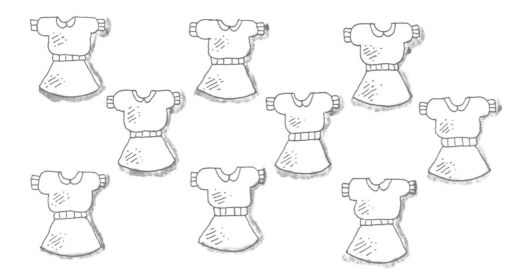

Using Multiple Relationships to Find Combinations

Practice your writing skills for numbers 21 through 100.

Make up your own addition problems and solve.

Make up your own subtraction problems and solve.

Enrichment
Reading Grade 1

AMERICAN
EDUCATION
PUBLISHING

My Clown

Make the clowns the same.

Draw what is missing on the second clown.

Is It the Same?

Play this with a grown-up.

Toss a penny on the Game Board.

Look at the drawing under your penny.

If you have the same drawing on your Playing
Card, cross it out.

Take turns.

You win if you cross out all your drawings first.

Game Board

My Playing Card

My Grown-up's Playing Card

2 ▶ To the Doghouse

Help the dog get home.

Draw a path from the dog to its home.

Do not cross over any lines.

Doghouse

It Moved

Do this with a grown-up.
Put a spoon, a fork, and a knife
on a table.
Close your eyes.
Have your grown-up move one thing.
Open your eyes.
Which thing was moved?
If you know, you may color a star.
Play 6 rounds.

Round 1   Round 2   Round 3

Round 4   Round 5   Round 6

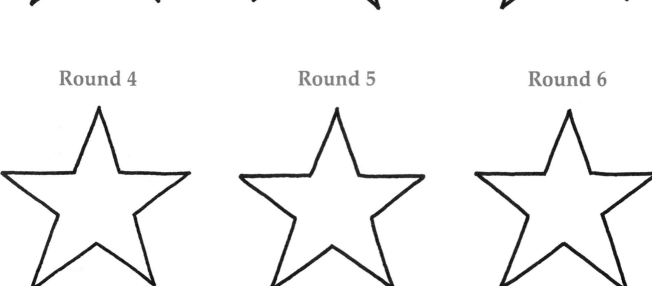

3   Rhyme Design

Look at the circle.

Draw lines between things
with names that rhyme.

Trace over the one done for you.

Then do the rest.

Color the shapes you made in the circle.

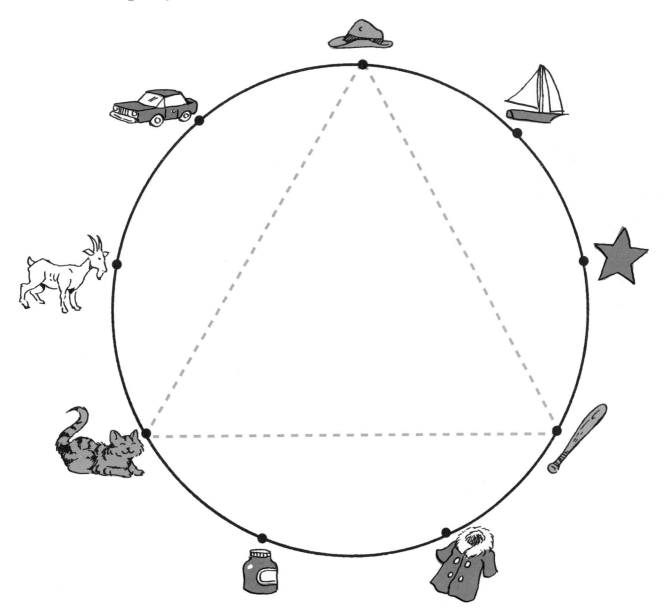

Orders

Do this with a grown-up.

Have your grown-up read each set of orders.

Then try to follow the orders exactly.

If you make a mistake, have your grown-up read the orders again and you try again.

You have 3 chances for each set of orders.

Orders

Jump three times. Then walk in a circle. Did you do it? _____	Sit on the floor. Then clap your hands. Did you do it? _____
Clap two times. Then touch your feet. Did you do it? _____	Stand on one foot. Then take three little hops. Did you do it? _____
Rub your head two times. Then touch your nose. Did you do it? _____	Pull on your ear. Then pull on your hair. Did you do it? _____
Turn in a circle. Then stamp your foot. Then wiggle your fingers. Did you do it? _____	Make a silly face. Then hum a tune. Then touch your toes. Did you do it? _____

Sounds, Sounds

Say the name of each picture.
Listen to the first sound you hear in the name.
Find 3 pictures with names that begin with
the same first sound.
Circle the letter under each of the 3 pictures.

   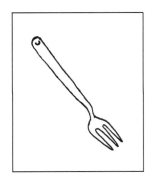      

y   n   e   o

k   t   s   r

Do this to find out if you are right.
  Write the 3 letters you circled.
  Write them in order here.

_____   _____   _____

If you are right, the letters spell a great word.

In My Home

Do this with a grown-up.
Look around your home.

Mitt begins with the same sound as **moon**.

Find something that begins with the same sound as <u>run</u>.

Find something that begins with the same sound as <u>ball</u>.

Write its name. _____

Write its name. _____

Draw a picture of what you named.

Draw a picture of what you named.

Find something that ends with the same sound as <u>wet</u>.

Find something that ends with the same sound as <u>good</u>.

Write its name. _____

Write its name. _____

Draw a picture of what you named.

Draw a picture of what you named.

Developing auditory awareness of consonant sounds

5 ▶ The Farm

Look at the picture on this page.
Find 5 things with names that begin with
the same sound as <u>fall</u>.
Color them blue.

Find 5 things with names that begin with
the same sound as <u>day</u>.
Color them yellow.

Find 5 things with names that begin with
the same sound as <u>ten</u>.
Color them red.

Do this with a grown-up.

Help the Green family pack for a trip.

Take turns.

Draw a line from each person to things
he or she will pack.

Mom will pack things with names that begin with
the same sound as <u>mop</u>.

Dad will pack things with names that begin with
the same sound as <u>pig</u>.

Pat will pack things with names that end with
the same sound as <u>look</u>.

Bill will pack things with names that end with
the same sound as <u>well</u>.

6 ▸ Tic-Tac-Toe

Look at each box in the Tic-Tac-Toe game.
Read the word and say the name
of the picture.
If the word names the picture, color the box.
When you are finished you will have tic-tac-toe.

Tic-Tac-Toe

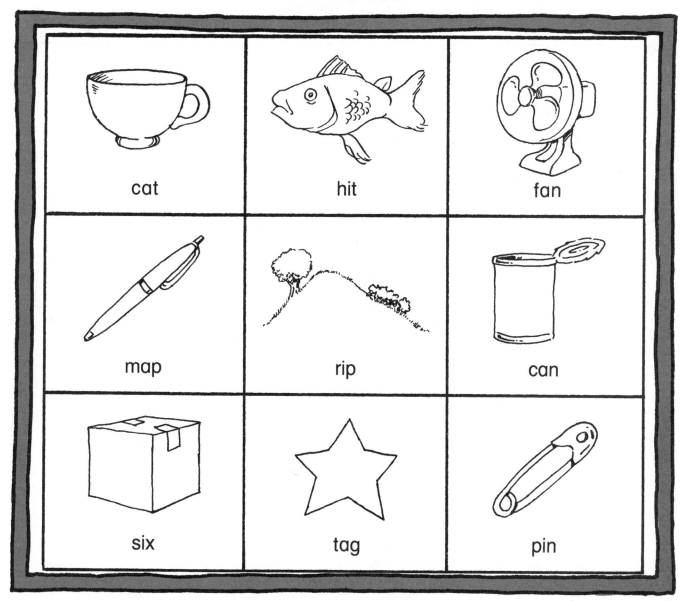

cat	hit	fan
map	rip	can
six	tag	pin

Toss a Word

Play this game with a grown-up.

Get a penny and toss it on the game board.

Look at the letter in the space where the penny lands.

Try to use the letter to finish a word on your
Word Card.

Write the letter in the word.

Take turns.

To win, you must fill in your Word Card first.

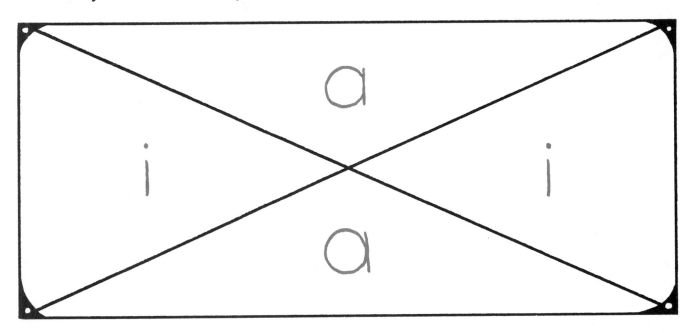

My Word Card

l____p   d____g   r____b   c____p   f____n   m____p

My Grown-up's Word Card

l____p   d____g   r____b   c____p   f____n   m____p

Name _____   **Reading Grade 1**

 Word Hunt

Look at each box below.

Name the picture and read the two words.

Circle the word that names the picture.

Then find the word in the Word Hunt.

The word may go across or down.

Circle the word.

The first one is done for you.

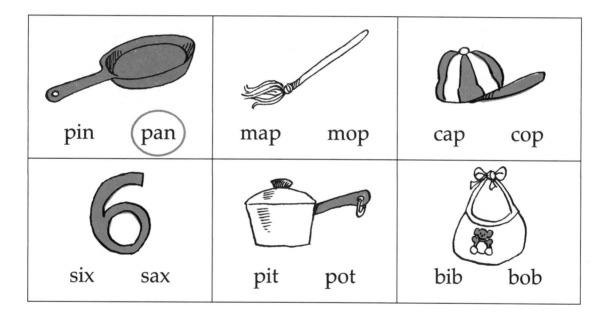

pin (pan)	map mop	cap cop
six sax	pit pot	bib bob

Word Hunt

s	i	x	m	c	p
v	k	i	p	a	o
m	o	p	a	p	t
b	i	b	n	c	a

Reading words with short *a*, *i*, and *o*   **155**

Make a Word

Play this game with a grown-up.
Make letter cards like these.

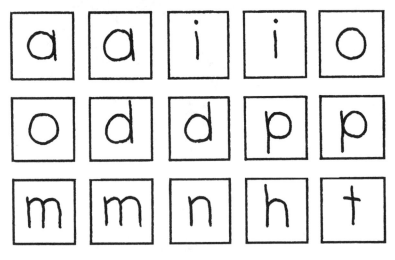

Turn over the cards.

Pick 3 cards.

Try to use the letters to make a real word.

Write the word on your Word Board.

Then turn your cards back over.

Take turns.

The first player to make 3 different words wins.

My Word Board	My Grown-up's Word Board

Silly Drawings

Read each sentence and do what it says.

Draw a sad pig in a big box.

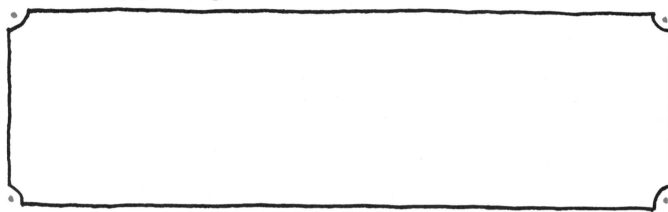

Draw a pup in a tub full of mud.

Draw six big wet bugs in a cup.

Do They Sound the Same?

Play this game with a grown-up.
Make word cards like these.

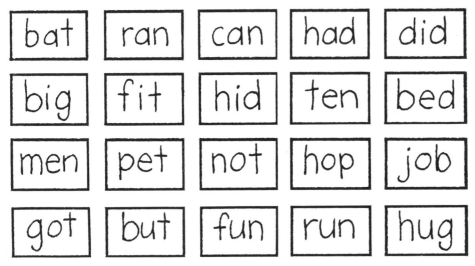

bat	ran	can	had	did
big	fit	hid	ten	bed
men	pet	not	hop	job
got	but	fun	run	hug

Turn over the cards.

Pick 2 cards.

Read the words on the cards out loud.

Listen for the vowel sounds.

If the words have the same vowel sound,
keep the cards.

If the words do not have the same vowel sound,
turn the cards back over.

Take turns.

Play until no more cards are left.

Then count your cards.

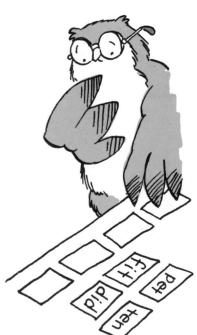

How many cards do you have? _____

How many cards does your grown-up have? _____

The player with more cards wins the game.

⑨ Word Stars

Look at the 3 word beginnings next to the first star.

Now look at the word endings in the star.

Pick a beginning for each ending.

Write it on the line.

Trace over the one done for you.

Then do the rest the same way.

bl   fl   cl

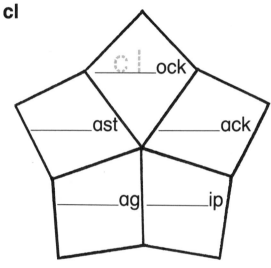

_____cl_ock

_____ast   _____ack

_____ag   _____ip

sl   tr   fr

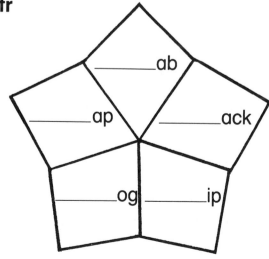

_____ab

_____ap   _____ack

_____og   _____ip

Beginnings and Endings

Play this game with a grown-up.

You will put together word beginnings and endings.

Toss a coin.

If the coin lands heads up, you may make 1 word.

If the coin lands tails up, you may make 2 words.

Write your words on your Word Card.

Take turns.

The first player to fill a Word Card wins.

I'll use **bl** and **ock**. That makes the word **block**!

Word Beginnings

bl   sl   cl   fl

gr   dr   tr   st

Word Endings

ip   ock   ap   am   ob

ab   ill   ub   ick   ess

My Word Card

_____

_____

_____

_____

_____

My Grown-up's Word Card

_____

_____

_____

_____

_____

10 Hidden Message

Look at each picture and say its name.
Listen for the beginning sound.
Color the box if the name begins with the same
sound as <u>chin</u>, <u>shoe</u>, or <u>thumb</u>.
When you finish, the colored boxes will make a word.

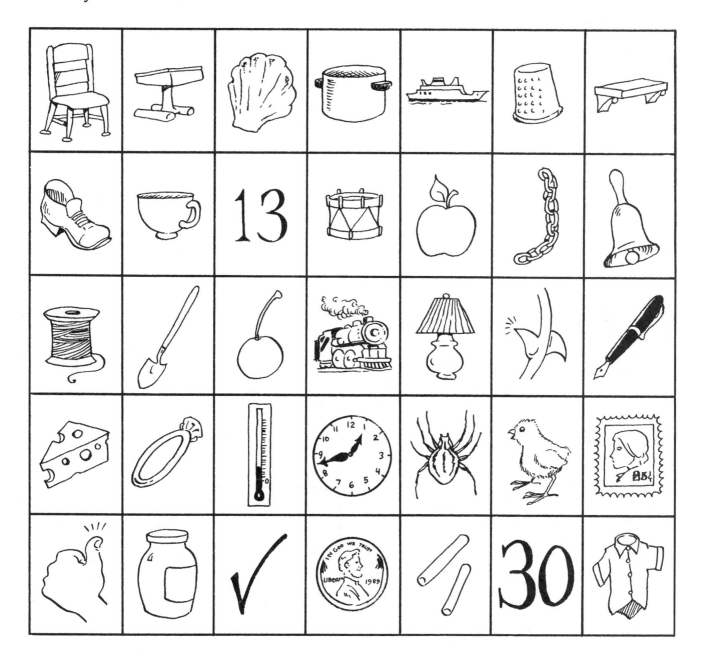

Down the Road

Play this game with a grown-up.

Make letter cards like these.

Turn over the cards.

Then get a small marker for each player.

Put the markers on GO.

Take turns picking a card.

Look at the letters on the card.

Move your marker to the next picture with a name that begins with the sound the letters stand for.

Then turn the card back over.

Play until one player lands on the last picture.

Play the game 3 or more times.

The winner is the player who lands on the last picture more often.

11 ▷ They Are Hiding

There are 7 things hiding in the picture.
Each thing is named in the Word Box.
Read all the words in the Word Box.
Then try to find the things in the picture.
Color the things you find.

Word Box

kite	bone
cape	cane
flute	mule
pine cone	

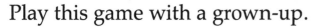

Word Boxes

Play this game with a grown-up.

Pick 3 boxes.

Write an **e** at the end of each word in your boxes.

Read the new words.

Score 1 point for each real word.

Keep score on a piece of paper.

Have your grown-up do the rest of the boxes.

Box 1

bit _____

pot _____

cap _____

Box 2

tap _____

cut _____

fun _____

Box 3

hop _____

rob _____

rip _____

Box 4

fin _____

kit _____

box _____

Box 5

pin _____

not _____

rid _____

Box 6

pet _____

mud _____

lot _____

Who scored more points? _____

12 ▸ Who Is the Winner?

Who will be the winner?
Each child has a word card.
Add an **e** to the end of each word.
Read the new word.

The winner does not have a real word.

Who is the winner? _____

Word Wheel

Play this game with a grown-up.

Make letter cards like these.

Turn over the cards.

Pick a card.

Try to use the letter or letters to finish a word on your Word Wheel.

Write the letter or letters that finish the word.

Then turn over the card.

Take turns.

You win if you fill in your Word Wheel first.

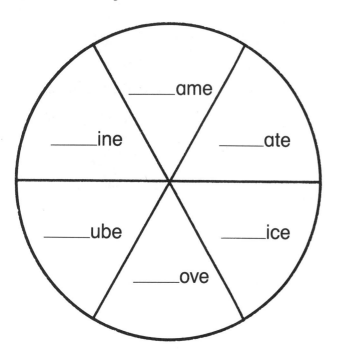

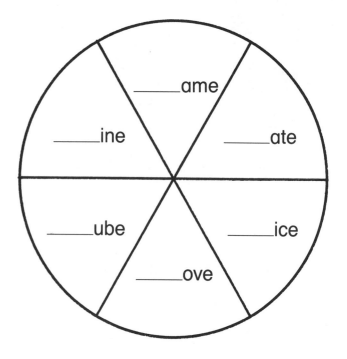

My Word Wheel

____ame
____ate
____ice
____ove
____ube
____ine

My Grown-up's Word Wheel

____ame
____ate
____ice
____ove
____ube
____ine

13 ▶ Like It or Not

Read all the words in the box.
Circle every word that names something you like.
Put an **X** on every word that names something
you do not like.

rabbits	kites	parks	walking
apples	bears	bread	dolls
ball	milk	mice	playing
toys	cats	dogs	running
singing	zoos	trees	birds

Write the names of other places, foods, animals, things to do, or playthings you like.

_____

_____

_____

Write the names of other places, foods, animals, things to do, or playthings you do not like.

_____

_____

_____

Word Boxes

Play this game with a grown-up.
Make number cards like these.
Turn over the cards.
Pick a card.
Find the number on the card in the
Word List.
Read the word out loud.
If the word is in your Word Box, put an **X** on it.
If the word is not in your Word Box, turn the
card back over.
Take turns.
You win if you cross out all the words in your
Word Box first.

1	2	3	4	5
6	7	8	9	
10	11	12		

Word List

1. did	**4.** him	**7.** look	**10.** find
2. eat	**5.** could	**8.** after	**11.** who
3. was	**6.** your	**9.** put	**12.** good

My Word Box

good	was
eat	did
your	put

My Grown-up's Word Box

him	look
could	after
find	who

14 Label Me

Look at the picture.
Then read the words in the
Word Box.
Use the words in the Word Box to
label the things in the picture.
Trace over the label for <u>floor</u>.
Then do the rest.

Word Box

chair	rug	floor
toys	bed	wall
	window	

Do this with a grown-up.

Read these 6 words.

bunny   they   from   all   party   day

Now make up a little story for your grown-up.
Use as many of the 6 words as you can.

How many of the words did you use? _____

Let your grown-up have a turn.
Your grown-up must make up a new story.

How many of the words did your grown-up use? _____

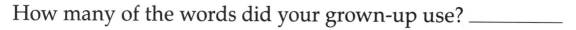

Try again with these 7 words.

down   up   water   you   more   little   ask

How many of the words did you use? _____

How many of the words did your grown-up use? _____

Now try with these 8 words.

light   name   fire   very   come   bear   girl   boy

How many of the words did you use? _____

How many of the words did your grown-up use? _____

15 ▷ Zoo or Farm?

Read the story.

Each time you come to 2 words, circle the one
you want in the story.

My Story

My   mother / father   went to a   zoo / farm   .   I went too.   So did

my   sister / brother   .   We went by   bus / car   .   On the way I

saw a   bear / dog   .   It was   big / small   .   I said, "I want

to   help / have   it.   My   mom / dad   said I   could / could not   .

What will happen now?

Draw a picture or write your idea.

Use another sheet of paper.

Word Checkers

Play this game with a grown-up.

Make 8 small red markers.

Put them on the two bottom rows of words.

Have your grown-up make 8 small blue markers.

Put them on the two top rows of words.

Then play checkers, but with one difference.

Read the word in a box before you put a marker on it.

	to		do		has		of
let		as		so		fly	
	us		for		be		old
two		now		who		way	
	get		me		by		yes
up		had		her		him	
	but		old		saw		day

16 ▷ Find the One

Read the 4 words in this box.
Three of the words go together.
Put an **X** on the word that does
not go with the other words.

cow	chicken
pig	sky

Try again with the words in these boxes.

red	blue
fish	yellow

girl	house
boy	woman

goat	chair
table	desk

ant	bee
fly	grass

Now make up your own set
of 4 words.

Make sure 3 of the words go
together.

The last word should not go
with the 3 other words.

Which Is Better?

Do this with a grown-up.

Read the words in the first box.

Put an **X** under the name of the thing you like better.

Put a ✔ under the name of the thing your grown-up likes better.

Do the rest of the boxes the same way.

apple or banana	milk or juice	lions or tigers

elephants or bears	trees or flowers	winter or summer

airplanes or trains	cars or trucks	orange or green

Make up 2 more sets of words.

Put an **X** under the names of the things you like better.

_____ or _____   _____ or _____

7 It's a Fact

How big is a baby kangaroo when it is born?
Here is how to find out.
Read each set of words.
If both words mean the same or almost
the same thing, circle the set.

cut   paint

fast   quick

talk   speak

right   pen

see   look

keep   save

sun   eat

always   never

How many circles did you make? _____
If you made 5 circles, a baby kangaroo can fit in a cup.
If you made 4 circles, it can fit on a thumbnail.
If you made 3 circles, it can fit in a shoe.

Fill the Balloons

Play this game with a grown-up.

Toss a coin on the game board.

Read the words in the box where the coin lands.

If the words have the same or almost the same meaning, color 2 of your balloons.

If the words have opposite meanings, color 1 balloon.

Take turns.

You win if you color all your balloons first.

happy sad	on off	little small	more less
nice mean	silly funny	up down	below under

My Balloons

My Grown-up's Balloons

18 ▸ A Riddle

Find the mystery number.

It is the number that belongs on the next 2 lines.

The number after 8 is _____.

$5 + 4 =$ _____.

What is the mystery number? _____

Find the mystery word.

It is the word that belongs on the next 2 lines.

I gave Joe 50 _____ to buy a pencil.

The toy costs 2 dollars and 30 _____.

What is the mystery word? _____

Now here is a riddle for you.

What is the difference between an old penny and a new dime?

The answer is the mystery number and the mystery word.

Write them below to answer the riddle.

Mystery Number   **Mystery Word**

_____   _____

Lost Words

Work with a grown-up
to finish the story.
Take turns putting the lost
words back in the story.
Use words from the Word Box.

Word Box

eyes	bed	asleep
into	hug	friend
tree	sky	up
	Squirrel	

Bedtime

"It is time for bed, Little Squirrel," said Mother Squirrel.

Little Squirrel said, "I want to stay _____.

I want to climb the big oak _____. I want to

visit my _____ the frog."

"Not tonight, Little _____. The moon is high

in the _____. It is time for _____."

Mother Squirrel gave Little Squirrel a big _____.

She tucked him _____ bed. Little Squirrel closed

his _____ and fell _____.

Name the Pictures

Look at the pictures.

Give each picture a name.

Pick a name from the Name Box.

Write the name under the picture.

Name Box

The Picnic	The Party
A New Pup	Turtle Time

What Is Happening?

Look at this picture with a grown-up.
Talk about what is happening.

Now talk with your grown-up about these questions.

Where do you think the boy and his dad are going?

What stops them?

What do you think the boy says to his dad?

What do you think Dad says to the boy?

Give the picture a name.

My name for the picture is _____

_____.

My grown-up's name for the picture is _____

_____.

20 Puppy Puppet

This is how to make a puppy puppet.
You need an envelope, a scissors, and a pencil.

1. Close the envelope.

2. Cut a strip from the long side of the envelope.

3. Fold the envelope in half.

4. Draw a puppy's eyes, nose, and mouth
on the top of the folded envelope.

5. Put your fingers in the top opening of the envelope.
Put your thumb in the bottom.

6. Play with your puppy puppet.

Pick Up the Ice

Do this with a grown-up.
Get an ice cube, a glass of water,
a piece of thread, and some salt.

Now you will use the piece of thread
to pick up the ice cube from the
glass of water.
You will not touch the ice with
your fingers.
Just do these things and it will be
easy to lift the ice cube.

ice cube

glass of water

piece of thread

salt

1. Put a new ice cube into the
   glass of water.

2. Dip one end of the thread
   into the water.

3. Lay the wet end of the thread
   across the top of the ice.

4. Shake salt on top of the ice cube
   and thread.

5. Let the thread stay on the top of
   the ice cube for 1 minute.
   Now slowly pull up on the thread.

21 ▶ Work Tools

Pretend you are a doctor.
Write 3 things you need for your job.

_____

_____

_____

Pretend you are a carpenter.
Write 3 things you need for your job.

_____

_____

_____

Pretend you are a teacher.
Write 3 things you need for your job.

_____

_____

_____

Fill the Lists

Do this with a grown-up.

Look at the Word Board.

Take turns writing words in the lists.

Choose 2 lists on each turn.

Write 1 word in each list.

Score 2 points if your word ends a list.

Keep score on a piece of paper.

The winner is the player with more points.

GAMES ? FOODS ?

Word Board

Games	Colors	Animals
_____	_____	_____
_____	_____	_____
_____	_____	_____
_____	_____	_____

Foods	Clothes	Numbers
_____	_____	_____
_____	_____	_____
_____	_____	_____

22 ▸ At the Zoo

Look at the picture.

The zoo animals are sad.

They talk to the zoo keeper.

What will the zoo keeper do now?

Write your idea.

Do not worry about spelling.

Just do your best.

_____

_____

_____

What Now?

Do this with a grown-up.
Look at the picture.

What is happening?

My grown-up thinks _____

_____.

What will happen next?

I think _____

_____.

Party Time

Pretend you and your best friends
want to have a party.
Plan a Best Friends Party.
Do not worry about spelling.
Just do your best.

Party Plans

Write 2 things you will do before the party.

_____

_____

Write 2 things you will do at the party.

_____

_____

Write 2 things you will do after the party.

_____

_____

The Right Order

Do this with a grown-up.

There are 4 stories on the page.

Take turns tossing a coin.

If the coin lands heads up, you read a story out loud.

If the coin lands tails up, your grown-up reads a story out loud.

Play until all the stories are read.

Story 1

Sue ate breakfast.

She woke up.

She went to school.

Story 2

Bill put on his shoes.

He put on his shirt.

He put on his socks.

Story 3

Jill liked the red flower.

She wanted the red flower.

She saw a man with flowers.

Story 4

Tom went to the store.

He got milk and apples.

He paid for the food.

Now answer this question.

Which story do you think

tells things in the right order?　**Story** _____

Turn the page upside down to check your answer.

How many ears do 2 rabbits have altogether? _____
The answer is the number of the story that
is in the right order.

24 ⟩ Tim Bear

The Tim Bear is a new toy.

Look at this ad for a Tim Bear.

Tim Bear Is the Best Bear!

　　Tim is soft.

　　Tim can talk.

　　Tim can sing.

Tim is sold only at the Fun Time Toy Store.

　Get Tim on Monday and save **$1.00**

Circle the answer to each question.

Can Tim talk?	YES	NO
Can Tim walk?	YES	NO
Can you get Tim at the Super Toy Store?	YES	NO
Can you get Tim at the Fun Time Toy Store?	YES	NO
Can you get Tim on Monday?	YES	NO
Would you like to get Tim?	YES	NO

Do this with a grown-up.

Look at the picture for as long as you want.

Then cover the picture.

Work with your grown-up to answer the questions.

How many people are in the store? _____

How many children are in the store? _____

How many dolls are on the shelf? _____

Name 2 other toys in the store. _____

_____

What toy is each child holding? _____

25 ▷ Plans, Plans

Rosa and Roy have plans.
Read each set of plans.
Look for 2 things Roy or Rosa must
do before the plan can come true.
Draw a line under each thing.

The Plans

Roy wants to read a book.

1. He must pick out a book.
2. He must stand on his hands.
3. He must open up the book.

Rosa wants to swim.

1. She must put on a swim suit.
2. She must go to the pool.
3. She must draw a picture.

Rosa wants to cook an egg.

1. She must call her friend.
2. She must get a pan.
3. She must crack the egg.

Roy wants a flower garden.

1. He must get flower seeds.
2. He must eat 2 carrots.
3. He must water the seeds.

Look at the numbers next to the sentences
you underlined.
Write the numbers here.

___ + ___ + ___ + ___ + ___ + ___ + ___ + ___ = _____

Now add the numbers.
Your answer should be 16.

Why Did It Happen?

Do this with a grown-up.

Read each sentence in dark print.

Think about what it says.

Then answer the question about what happened.

Your answer may be silly or not silly.

Latoya's dog barked and barked.

What happened to make Latoya's dog bark?

I think _____

_____.

My grown-up thinks _____

_____.

David ran home as fast as he could.

What happened to make David run home?

I think _____

_____.

My grown-up thinks _____

_____.

26 ▶ Name the Person

Think of real people, storybook people,
and people on TV.
Use their names when you answer
these questions.

Who likes comic books?

_____

Who likes computer games?

_____

Who likes the same foods as you?

_____

Whom would you trust with a secret?

_____

Whom do you like to be with
when you feel silly?

_____

Whom do you like to be with
when you feel sleepy?

_____

A Helping Hand

Read this story with a grown-up.

Grandmother

Grandmother doesn't feel well. She feels sad, too. Julio and his mom are going to visit Grandmother. On the way, they want to buy four things to help Grandmother feel better and happier. What should they buy?

Write 2 things you think Julio and his mom should buy for Grandmother.

_____

_____

Have your grown-up write 2 things Julio and his mom should buy for Grandmother.

_____

_____

27 The Moon

Read this story about the moon.

The Moon

What makes the moon shine? The moon shines because of the sun. Light from the sun hits the moon and makes the moon glow. The moon shines all day and all night. We only see the shining moon at night when it is dark on Earth.

Now read the 2 sentences in dark print.
Draw a line under the sentence that tells
what the story is mostly about.

The moon is very big.   **The sun makes the moon shine.**

April, 1950   July, 1969

Look at the date under the sentence you underlined.
If you underlined the right sentence, you found the
date when a person first walked on the moon.

You can check your answer.
Just turn your book upside down and read the sentence.

A person first walked on the moon in July, 1969.

What's It About?

Do this with a grown-up.
Here are 2 stories.
Each of you read your story out loud.

My Story

Marta likes her baby sister.
The baby sleeps a lot. She eats a
lot. She cries a lot. But when she
sees Marta, she smiles a lot.

My Grown-up's Story

Don likes to cook. He can
make toast. He can make soup.
Once he even made a pizza. Don
makes really great food. He is a
very good cook.

Now look at the Game Board.
Read all the sentences out loud.
Then take turns.
Toss a penny on the Game Board.
Try to land on the sentence that tells
what your story is mostly about.
You win if you land on your sentence first.

Game Board

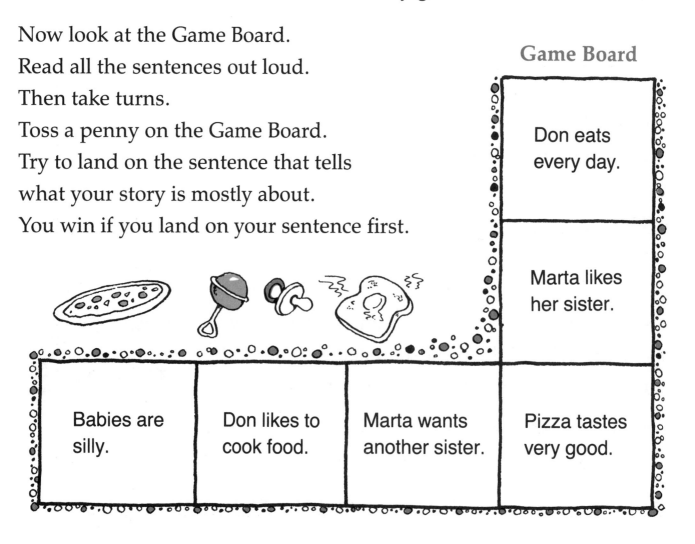

Don eats
every day.

Marta likes
her sister.

Babies are
silly.

Don likes to
cook food.

Marta wants
another sister.

Pizza tastes
very good.

Picture the Story

ead this story.

Fluff is a happy cat. She lives with a good family. Molly is . She loves to pet Fluff. Josh 10. He feeds Fluff. Mom is ice, too. She brushes Fluff.
Everything is fine until the amily comes home with a dog. luff does not want a dog.

The dog walks up to Fluff. Fluff is afraid. Fluff wants to run away. The dog licks Fluff. It feels good. Fluff licks the dog. Fluff and the dog start to play. Fluff is happy again. It is nice to have a dog for a pal. Molly, Josh, and Mom are happy, too.

Color the picture that goes with the story.

Name the Animals

Play this game with a grown-up.

Pick an animal from the Animal List.

Think about how the animal looks and acts.

Then tell your grown-up about the animal.

DO NOT tell the name of the animal.

Score 1 point if your grown-up names the animal.

Take turns.

Play 5 rounds.

Write your points on your score cards.

The winner is the player with more points.

Animal List

cat	pig	bear	lion	sheep	spider
wolf	fly	goat	horse	mouse	elephant
dog	cow	bird	tiger	hamster	squirrel

My Score Card	My Grown-up's Score Card
Round 1 _____	Round 1 _____
Round 2 _____	Round 2 _____
Round 3 _____	Round 3 _____
Round 4 _____	Round 4 _____
Round 5 _____	Round 5 _____
Total _____	Total _____

29 > My Favorites

Write about your favorite things.
Do not worry about spelling. Just do your best.

My Favorite Things

My favorite time of year is _____.

I like it best because _____

_____.

My favorite holiday is _____.

I like it best because _____

_____.

My favorite game is _____.

I like it best because _____

_____.

My favorite story is _____.

I like it best because _____

_____.

Who Was First?

Do this with a grown-up.
Read each story out loud with your grown-up.
Your grown-up may help you with names.
Have your grown-up guess whom the story is about.
Draw a line under the name of your grown-up's guess.

Story 1

I made the first American flag. I used stars and stripes. Who am I?

Paul Revere

Betsy Ross

Story 2

I was the first African-American to be named a Supreme Court Judge. Who am I?

Rosa Parks

Thurgood Marshall

Story 3

I was the first First Lady of the United States. George and I never lived in the city of Washington, D.C. Who am I?

Martha Washington

Jane Adams

Story 4

I made the first light bulb. I also made the first record player and the first movie. Who am I?

Thomas A. Edison

Alexander Graham Bell

Now check your answers.

ANSWERS

Story 4 Thomas A. Edison

Story 3 Martha Washington

Story 2 Thurgood Marshall

Story 1 Betsy Ross

Three Poems

Read these poems.

Polar Bear

The secret of the polar bear
Is that he wears long underwear.

                    Gail Kredenser

Oodles of Noodles

I love noodles. Give me oodles.
Make a mound up to the sun.
Noodles are my favorite foodles.
I eat noodles by the ton.

        Lucia and James L. Hymes, Jr.

HOW TO BE SERIOUS

Catch a smile

from a clown

and quickly turn it

upside down

now look

you've got

a lovely

frown.

                    Eve Merriam

Draw a picture to go with the poem you like best.

Our Poem

Finish the poem with a grown-up.
The poem may be silly or not silly.
Use words from your Word Lists.
You finish every line with ★.
Your grown-up finishes every line with ★★★.
Read the poem out loud when you are finished.

I can rhyme all the time.

My Word List				
win	fin	in	grin	twin
pin	tin	thin	skin	spin

My Grown-up's Word List				
bay	day	hay	say	play
jay	pay	ray	clay	gray

★★★ Once a blue _____

★★★ all dressed in _____,

   ★ wanted to _____

   ★ at night on a _____.

★★★ It saw some _____,

★★★ it went to _____,

   ★ when suddenly a _____

   ★ said, "I want to _____."

31 ▶ Who Will Help?

Read this story.

Who Will Help?

Once a hen found a wheat seed. "Who will help me plant the seed?" she asked.

"Not I," said the duck.

"Not I," said the dog.

"Then I will do it myself," said the hen. And she did.

When the wheat was fully grown, the hen said, "Who will help cut the wheat and turn it to flour?"

"Not I," said the duck.

"Not I," said the dog.

"Then I will do it myself," said the hen. And she did.

When the flour was ready, the hen said, "Who will help me bake some bread?"

"Not I," said the duck.

"Not I," said the dog.

"Then I will do it myself," said the hen. And she did.

When the bread was done, the hen said, "Who will eat the bread?"

"I will," said the duck.

"I will," said the dog.

"No you will not!" said the hen. "I will eat it myself." And she did.

What lesson do you think the duck and the dog learned?

_____

_____

_____

After the Story Ends

Do this with a grown-up.
Read each story out loud.
Then finish the sentences about the story.

Goldilocks ran home as fast as she could go. She couldn't wait to see her mom. Goldilocks told her mom all about the 3 bears and their house in the woods. What did her mom say?

I think her mom said, "_____

_____."

My grown-up thinks her mom said, "_____

_____."

Jack cut the beanstalk. Down it came, giant and all. Jack went home with his pot of gold. He told his mother what he had done. What did his mother say?

I think his mother said, "_____

_____."

My grown-up thinks his mother said, "_____

_____."

Practice your writing skills.
Write the names of your family members.

Practice your writing skills.
Make a list of words that sound the same.

_____

_____

_____

_____

_____

_____

_____

_____

_____

_____

_____

_____

_____

Practice your writing skills.
Read one of your favorite stories out loud. Then write down the names of your favorite characters.

_____

_____

_____

_____

_____

_____

_____

_____

_____

_____

_____

_____

Enrichment
Reading Grade 2

AMERICAN
EDUCATION
PUBLISHING

1 Lost Letters

Write the lost letters in the box.
Make the word for the picture.

n [4] t

c [1 **o**] t    h [5] t

c [2] t    p [6] n

c [3] t    p [7] n

Match the numbers and write the lost letters in the boxes.
You will find out something great about yourself.

Y [**o**] [ ] [ ] r [ ] [ ] w [ ] nn [ ] r!
  1   2   3   4   5   6   7

Make a Word

Play this game with a grown-up.
Make consonant letter cards like these.

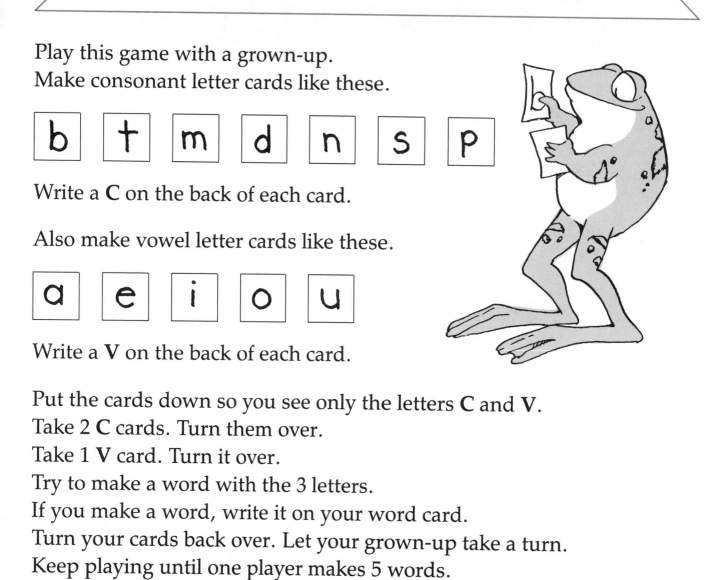

| b | t | m | d | n | s | p |

Write a **C** on the back of each card.

Also make vowel letter cards like these.

| a | e | i | o | u |

Write a **V** on the back of each card.

Put the cards down so you see only the letters **C** and **V**.
Take 2 **C** cards. Turn them over.
Take 1 **V** card. Turn it over.
Try to make a word with the 3 letters.
If you make a word, write it on your word card.
Turn your cards back over. Let your grown-up take a turn.
Keep playing until one player makes 5 words.

My Word Card	My Grown-up's Word Card

② Mystery Time

Can you solve a mystery?
Read the story.
Pick words to finish the story.
Find words with long vowel sounds and silent **e**.
Circle the words in the crime report.

Jane Kitty Cat has been robbed!

Her   toy / food / (rice)   is missing.

It was on the   floor. / stove. / wall.

The time was   two / five / four   o'clock.

The cat police came.
They looked in the house.

Police cat   Rose / Judd / Stan   found it.

It was in   Roy / Pete / Marta   Mouse's house.

The mouse was very sad and said,
"I will never rob again."

• OFFICIAL CAT POLICE •

Crime Report

What was missing?

rice _____

What time was the crime?

_____

Who was the robber?

_____

Who solved the crime?

_____

Is It a Word?

Play this game with a grown-up.
Make word cards like these.

kit __	tim __	top __	cap __	man __
rob __	tub __	pat __	cup __	cut __
fin __	tap __	not __	log __	box __

Pick a card and read the word.
Write an **e** on the end of the word.
Read your new word.
Is it a real word? Then write it on your word card.
Is it a nonsense word? Then you lose this turn.
Give your grown-up a chance.
You win if you fill in your word card first.

My Word Card	My Grown-up's Word Card
_____	_____
_____	_____
_____	_____
_____	_____

Yes or No

Cover the left side of the page.
Only look at the YES or NO side of the page.
On each line circle YES or NO.
Now read the questions on the left.
If your answer made sense, put a ✓ in the box.
If your answer did not make sense, put an **X** in the box.

	Cover This Side	**Pick YES or NO for Each Line**	
☐	Can a boat float?	YES	NO
☐	Can an apple seed read?	YES	NO
☐	Can it rain in Spain?	YES	NO
☐	Can you feel your heel?	YES	NO
☐	Can you drop a nail in a pail?	YES	NO
☐	Can a coat eat a goat?	YES	NO
☐	Can a toad hop down a road?	YES	NO
☐	Can a seal cook a meal?	YES	NO
☐	Can a slice of toast talk to a pot roast?	YES	NO
☐	Is meat a treat for a red beet?	YES	NO

How many of your answers made sense? _____

How many of your answers made no sense at all? _____

Toss a Word

Play this game with a grown-up.
Throw a penny or a paper clip on the game board.
Can you use the letters to make a word on your word card?
If you can, fill in the letters.
If not, you lose this turn.
If you land on **sorry**, you lose a turn.
Give your grown-up a turn.
You win if you finish the words on your word card first.

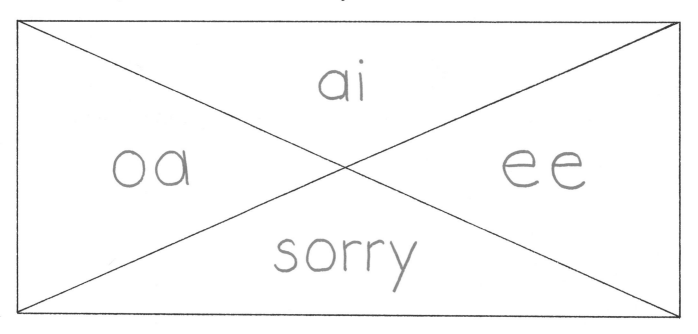

My Word Card	My Grown-up's Word Card
s _____ _____ p	s _____ _____ p
t _____ _____ d	t _____ _____ d
b _____ _____ t	b _____ _____ t
b _____ _____ p	b _____ _____ p
m _____ _____ n	m _____ _____ n

4 Hidden Words

Finish coloring every other letter in the puzzle.
Be sure you can still see the letters.

	g	b	r	l	e	u	e	e
n	l	g	e	r	a	a	v	s
e	s	s	i	o	n	n	a	a
t	p	a	i	l	n	l	k	g
t	l	r	a	e	s	e	s	

Write the colored letters in order.

b l u e

___ ___ ___ ___ ___ ___

___ ___   ___

___ ___ ___ ___

___ ___ ___

Draw a picture to match.

Write the other letters in order.

g r e e n

___ ___ ___ ___

___ ___   ___

___ ___ ___

___ ___ ___ ___ ___

Draw a picture to match.

Lotto

Play this game with a grown-up.
Make cards like these.

Turn over the cards.
Pick a card.
Try to use the letters on the card to make a word on
your lotto board.
Write the letters on your board and keep the card.
If you cannot make a word, turn the card back over.
Give your grown-up a turn.
You win if you fill in your lotto board first.

My Lotto Board	
_____ap	_____ape
_____im	_____ick
_____ope	_____op

My Grown-up's Lotto Board	
_____ack	_____iff
_____ick	_____ell
_____am	_____ip

5 ▶ Riddle Time

Try to solve these riddles.
Each answer begins with **ch**, **sh**, or **th**.

Riddle 1

I am in your home.
I am in your school.
I like tables.
Use me to give your feet a rest.

I am a _ch_____.

Riddle 2

You take me everywhere.
I am on your face.
I am under your lips.
I rhyme with win.

I am a _____.

Riddle 3

You also take me everywhere.
I am on your hand.
I like mittens.
I have a nail.

I am a _____.

Riddle 4

I float on water.
I am big.
People ride on me.
I go across the sea.

I am a _____.

Make up your own **ch**, **sh**, or **th** riddle.
Do not worry about spelling. Just do your best.

_____

_____

_____

_____

Tongue Twisters

Do this silly tongue twister with a grown-up.
Each of you try saying it three times FAST.

Ship   shape   thick   shake

Make up tongue twisters with your grown-up.
Each twister will have four words.
Each word begins with **ch**, **sh**, or **th**.
You finish the words. You may add an **s**.
Use words from the Tongue Twister Word Lists or
think of your own **ch**, **sh**, or **th** words.
Put a star next to the twister you like best.

Ship shape thiape shap thick...

Twister 1

Th_____   sh_____   th_____   ch_____

Twister 2

Ch_____   ch_____   sh_____   ch_____

Twister 3

Sh_____   sh_____   th_____   th_____

Tongue Twister Word Lists

ch words	**sh** words	**th** words
chip	shell	thick
chick	sheep	thin
chain	shine	think
change	sheet	three
chat	shoe	throw

6 ⟩ Trail of Nonsense

Can you get to the treasure?
Begin at START.
Read all the words in all the boxes.
Some of the words are real words.
Some of the words are nonsense words.
When you find a nonsense word, color the box.
When you are done, you will have a trail from
START to the treasure.

START

spork	dirm	sport	start	hard	hurt
smart	harb	larm	skird	bird	clerk
farm	born	fork	flerp	fort	form
star	card	merm	sark	spark	park
chirff	slorp	lurst	cart	firm	chart
lorp	march	pork	skirt	shirt	burn

TREASURE

Weave a Word

Work with a grown-up to make words.
Pick a letter or letters in column 1.
Draw a line first to **ar** and then to a letter in column 3.
If you make a real word or a name, write it in the word box.
Make 6 words, and you are a SUPER STAR.
Make 4 or 5 words, and you are a STAR BLAZER.
Two or 3 words are OK, but 0 or 1 word make you a FALLING STAR!

Column 1	Column 2	Column 3
b		n
p	ar	k
st		t

We made _____ words.

Word Box

barn _____

_____

_____

_____

_____

_____

Try with new letters.

Column 1	Column 2	Column 3
f		n
c	or	k
st		m

We made _____ words.

Word Box

_____

_____

_____

_____

_____

7 ▶ Hidden Picture

Read each word.
Color a word with a hard **c** sound BLACK.
Color a word with a soft **c** sound ORANGE.
Color a word that does not have a **c** sound BLUE.

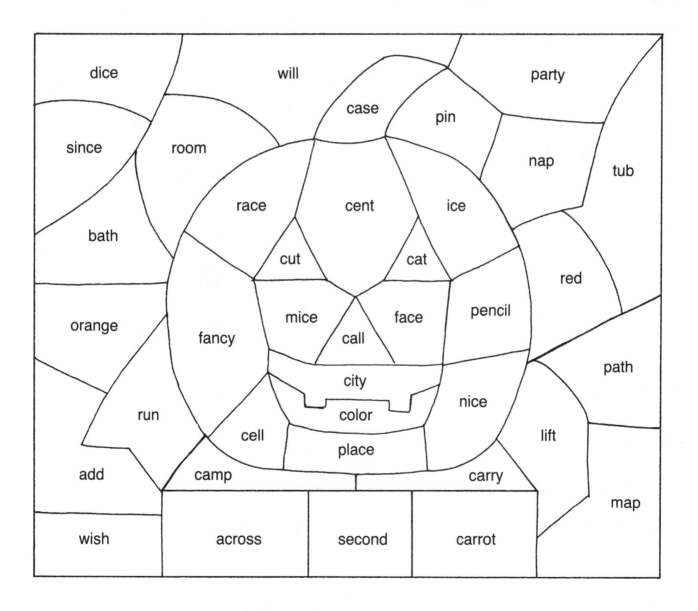

What is hidden in the picture? _____

Hard or Soft?

Play this game with a grown-up.
Throw the penny on the game board.
Read the word.
If the word has a hard **g** sound, you get 5 points.
If the word has a soft **g** sound, you get 10 points.
Let your grown-up have a turn.
Play 5 rounds. The higher score wins.

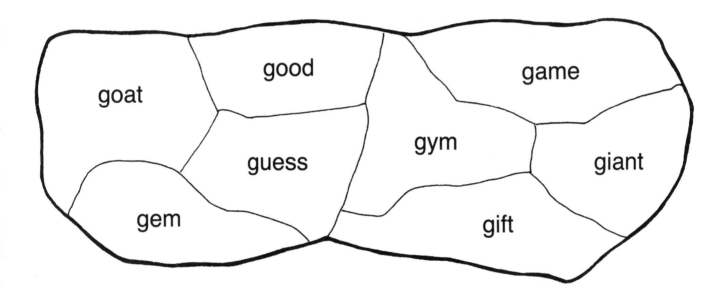

goat
good
game
guess
gym
giant
gem
gift

My Score Card	My Grown-up's Score Card
Round 1 _____	Round 1 _____
Round 2 _____	Round 2 _____
Round 3 _____	Round 3 _____
Round 4 _____	Round 4 _____
Round 5 _____	Round 5 _____
My Total _____	My Grown-up's Total _____

Ink Spots

Ink fell on the endings of some words on this page.
Read the story.
Put the ending **ed** or **ing** back on each word.
Remember, sometimes you must double the last
letter before adding an ending.

Best Friends

Ginny Mouse and Fred Mouse are best friends. They like
do_ing____ all the same things. They like play_____.
They like jump_____. They like eat_____ cheese.

One day Fred went to Ginny's for lunch. Ginny gave Fred
blue cheese. He want_____ Swiss cheese.

"I am go_____ home," shout_____ Fred.

Fred stamp_____ out of the mouse hole. He did not
know it, but a cat was watch_____ the hole. The cat saw
Fred leave the hole. She lick_____ her lips. "Mouse for
dinner!" she said.

Ginny saw the cat get_____ ready to jump. Ginny
scream_____, "Run, Fred! The cat is go_____ to get you."

Fred went run_____ back to the hole. Ginny took a broom
and smack_____ the cat's paw. The cat ran away.

Fred hug_____ Ginny and said, "You are my best friend."

Family Matters

Do this with a grown-up.
Name the oldest person living in your home. _____

Name the youngest person living in your home. _____

Name the tallest person living in your home. _____

Name the shortest person living in your home. _____

Have a contest with your grown-up.

Tiptoe across a room with
your grown-up. Who went slower? _____

Count to 50 with
your grown-up. Who counted faster? _____

Hold your breath with
your grown-up. Who held longer? _____

Draw a silly face.

Ask your grown-up to draw
a sillier face.

Work with your grown-up to
draw the silliest face of all.

Three of Everything

Make lists of things in your classroom or your home.
Do not worry about spelling. Just do your best.

List 3 things used for cooking.

_____

_____

_____

List 3 things you use every day.

_____

_____

_____

List 3 things that use electricity.

_____

_____

_____

List 3 things you sit on.

_____

_____

_____

List 3 things you can open.

_____

_____

_____

Tic-Tac-Toe Words

Play these tic-tac-toe games with a grown-up.
Play them just like all tic-tac-toe games.
Before you mark **X** or **O**, you must read the word.
If you cannot read the word, your grown-up will help you.
Play 4 rounds.

Round 1

other	more	people
long	only	animal
off	every	follow

Who won? _____

Round 2

who	where	could
must	again	right
away	house	from

Who won? _____

Round 3

around	land	change
turn	large	kind
want	old	because

Who won? _____

Round 4

need	before	us
high	next	air
found	school	eye

Who won? _____

Word Pictures

You can write a word to look like its meaning.
Look at these words.

little		
little		

mad

fat

Now it is your turn.
Read each word.
Write or draw the word so it looks like its meaning.

high	round

silly	fall

Word Road

Ask a grown-up to help you.
Put a penny on START.
Read the first word on the Word Road.
If you read it correctly, move to the second word.
Keep reading until you reach FINISH.
If you cannot read a word, your grown-up will read it for you.
Then you must return to START and begin all over again.
You have 4 chances to make the trip without your
grown-up reading a word.

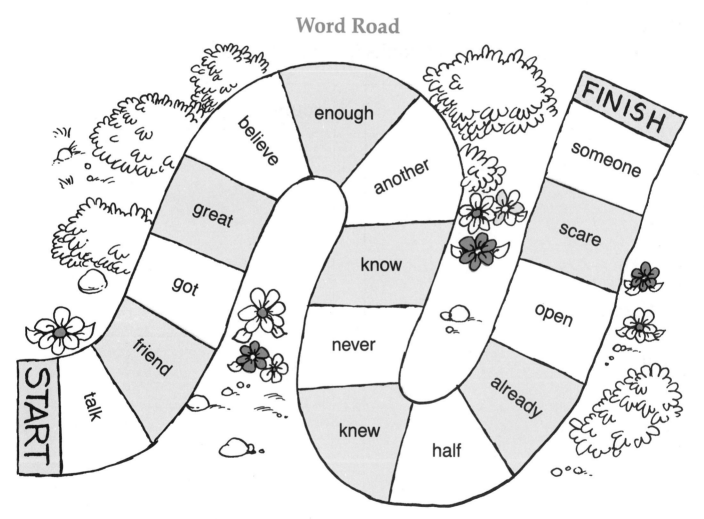

Word Road

Did you reach FINISH?

How many chances did it take you? _____

Name _____   **Reading Grade 2**

11 ▷ Word Hunt

Make the words below into compound words.
Use words from the box to make the
compound words.
Then hunt for the compound words
in the Word Hunt.
The words go across. The words go up and down.
Circle each compound word you find.

fish	yard	ball
town	box	top
paper	book	walk
chair	tub	shine

base_ **ball** _____   down _____   news_____

lunch _____   note_____   arm _____

side_____   sun _____   hill _____

gold_____   back _____   bath _____

Word Hunt

m	n	s	u	n	s	h	i	n	e	h
g	o	l	d	f	i	s	h	p	b	i
f	t	m	w	q	r	i	l	y	a	l
p	e	n	l	v	c	d	w	b	t	l
b	b	e	u	v	x	e	m	a	h	t
d	o	w	n	t	o	w	n	s	t	o
z	o	s	c	z	s	a	p	e	u	p
g	k	p	h	i	j	l	t	b	b	x
o	v	a	b	a	c	k	y	a	r	d
k	l	p	o	e	i	u	h	l	j	m
y	m	e	x	b	r	a	y	l	h	z
f	a	r	m	c	h	a	i	r	t	o

Compound Memory

Play this game with a grown-up.
Make word cards like these.

tool	box	foot	ball
pop	corn	air	plane
drive	way	week	end
home	work	fish	hook

up side

Turn over the cards.
Place them in even rows like this.

tooth

brush

Turn two cards face up.
If you can put the words together to make a real
compound word, keep the cards and pick again.
If you cannot make a compound word, turn the
cards back over.
Give your grown-up a chance.
Keep playing until all the cards are taken.
Whoever has more cards at the end wins the game.

12 ► Line Designs

Draw a line from the words to the contraction
that means the same.
When you finish, you will have some nice pictures
in the middle.

is not •   • he'll

we are •   • we're

he will •   • isn't

I will •   • didn't

have not •   • that's

they will •   • couldn't

could not •   • they'll

that is •   • haven't

did not •   • I'll

she is •   • you're

can not •   • can't

you are •   • she's

Star Bright

Play this game with a grown-up.
Make word cards like these.

| don't | you'll | he's | we'll | I'm |

| they're | it's | wasn't | aren't | she'll |

Turn over the cards.
Pick a card and read the contraction.
If your star has words that mean the same,
color that part of your star.
If you cannot make a match, turn the card back over.
Let your grown-up take a turn.
Keep playing until one player colors a whole star.

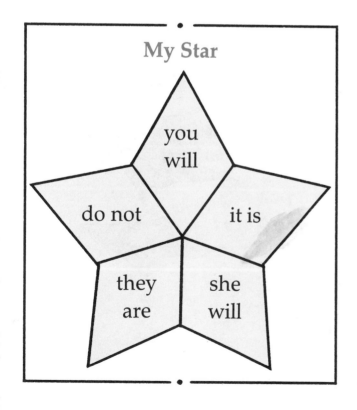

My Star

you will
do not
it is
they are
she will

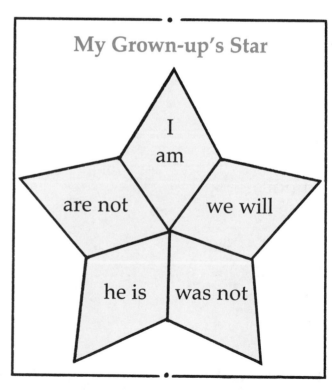

My Grown-up's Star

I am
are not
we will
he is
was not

13 ▸ Pretty As a Picture

You need a red crayon and a blue crayon.
Read the words in each part of the picture.
If the words have the same meaning, color the part RED.
If the words do not have the same meaning, color the part BLUE.

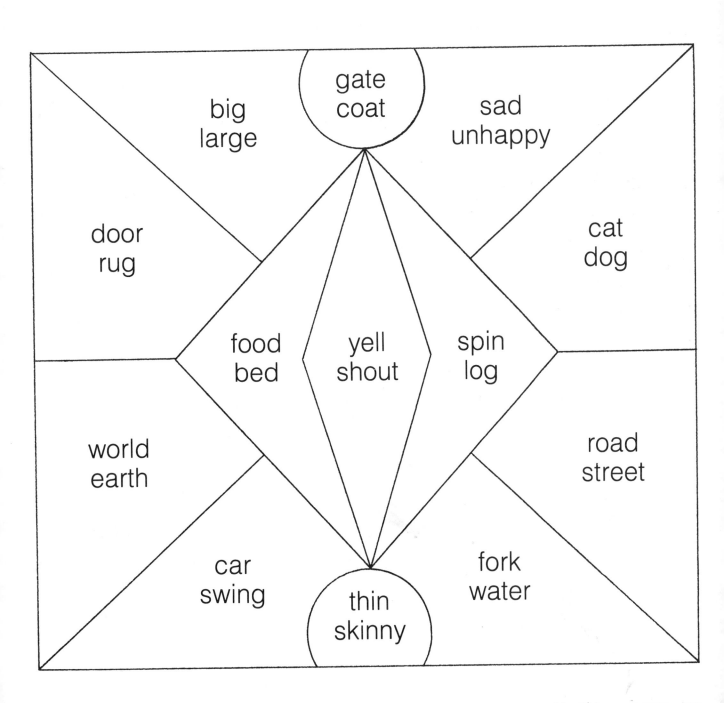

big
large

gate
coat

sad
unhappy

door
rug

cat
dog

food
bed

yell
shout

spin
log

world
earth

road
street

car
swing

thin
skinny

fork
water

Touchdown

Work with a grown-up on this page.
Here are 6 footballs.
The first football has the word **fast** on it.
You and your grown-up must think of 5 other
words that mean the same as **fast**.
Write each word on a football.
You get 10 points for each word you think of.
If you get 50 points you have made a touchdown!

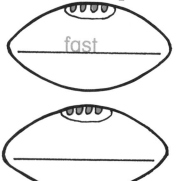 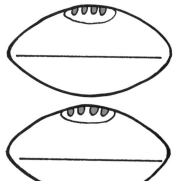 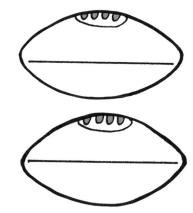

How many points did you get? _____
Did you make a touchdown? _____

Try again with a new set of footballs.
This time think of words that mean the same as **happy**.

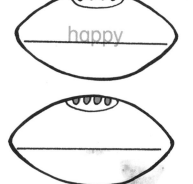 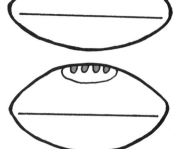 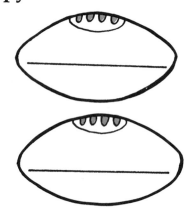

How many points did you get? _____
Did you make a touchdown? _____

14 Find the Mistakes

Here is Benny's homework paper.
Benny had to read each word on the paper.
He had to write a word that means the opposite.
Poor Benny, he made a lot of mistakes.
Correct his paper.
Mark ✓ next to each right answer.
Mark **X** next to each wrong answer.
For each wrong answer, change Benny's word.
Write a word that means the opposite of the word on the paper.

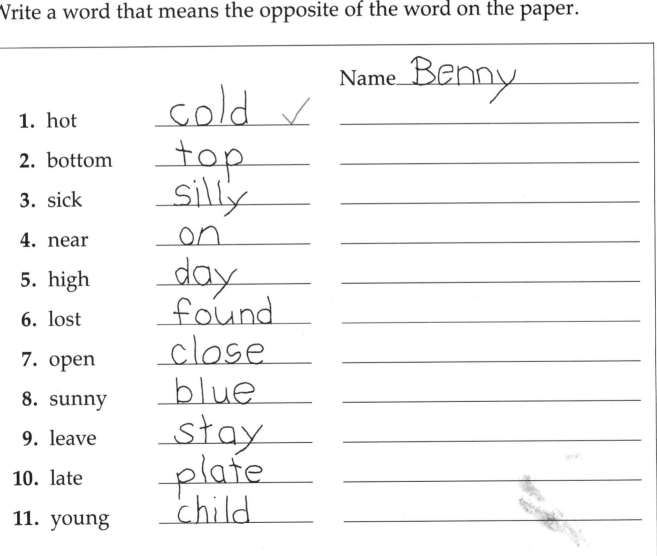

Name _Benny_____

1. hot   _cold_ ✓ _____

2. bottom   _top_ _____

3. sick   _silly_ _____

4. near   _on_ _____

5. high   _day_ _____

6. lost   _found_ _____

7. open   _close_ _____

8. sunny   _blue_ _____

9. leave   _stay_ _____

10. late   _plate_ _____

11. young   _child_ _____

Opposites

Play this game with a grown-up.
Have your grown-up read the words below out loud.
After you hear a word, say a word that means
the opposite.
If you are right, color a star.
If you are wrong, your grown-up colors a star.
The player with more colored stars wins.

head	all	empty
narrow	dirty	hard
frown	fake	gigantic
best	push	dangerous
rough	together	thick

My Stars

My Grown-up's Stars

15 ▷ The Long Sneeze

A person once sneezed for 150 days without stopping.

You can find out if this is true.
Look at the box filled with words.
You see each word 2 times.

bat	left	can	fan	rest	yard
bat	left	can	fan	rest	yard

Now read the sentences below.
Write a word from the box to finish each sentence.
Cross out each word after you use it.
When you are done, a word in the box will not be crossed out.
If that word has 4 letters, the sneeze story is true.
If that word has 3 letters, the sneeze story is not true.

It is hot. Turn on the _____.

I need my baseball _____.

The car must turn _____.

How many apples are _____ on the plate?

Where are the _____ of my toys?

Open a _____ of beans.

I _____ buy that robot.

I need a _____ of rope.

I worked hard and need to _____.

I am a rock-and-roll _____.

A _____ lives in a cave.

Which word was not crossed out? _____

Is the sneeze story true? _____

Riddle-De-Day

Try to make a grown-up laugh.
Read each riddle.
If your grown-up laughs, circle YES.
If your grown-up does not laugh, circle NO.

1. Question: Why is a river rich?
   Answer: Because it has two banks.   YES   NO

2. Question: Why is the cook mean?
   Answer: Because he beats the eggs and whips
           the cream.   YES   NO

3. Question: What did the rug say to the floor?
   Answer: Stick 'em up. I've got you covered.   YES   NO

4. Question: What has 18 legs and catches flies?
   Answer: A baseball team.   YES   NO

5. Question: When is a piece of wood like a king?
   Answer: When it is a ruler.   YES   NO

6. Question: What part of the fish weighs the
           most?
   Answer: The scales.   YES   NO

7. Question: Why did the basketball need a bib?
   Answer: Because it dribbled.   YES   NO

8. Question: What has a head, a tail, but no body?
   Answer: A penny.   YES   NO

16 ▸ Help the Writer

This story is not finished.
The writer left out a lot of words.
Help the writer finish the story.
Fill in the missing words.

Bessie and the Bird

One day Bessie was walking home from _____.

Suddenly, she saw a big _____ bird. Much to her

_____, the bird started to talk. The bird said, "I can show

you how to _____. Would you _____ that?"

"Oh yes," said Bessie.

The bird sprayed _____ dust on Bessie. Bessie felt

herself getting _____ and _____. It felt

_____. Bessie wished she could _____ all

day, but it was time to go _____.

The bird showed Bessie how to _____. Then the bird

asked, "Would you like me to come to see you _____?"

"Oh _____, please," said Bessie.

Everyday after _____ Bessie and the bird went

_____.

All Mixed Up

Do this with a grown-up.
Read each sentence.
The word in dark print is mixed up.
Figure out the mixed-up word.
Write it on the line at the end of the sentence.

1. What is **ti**? _____

2. I **nca** see you. _____

3. They like to **mjup** rope. _____

4. Can you see **vero** the fence? _____

5. Five comes after **rouf**. _____

6. A lot of **lppeoe** like to eat pizza. _____

Write the new words in order.
You will find out something true about a bullfrog.

___ ___   _____   ___ ___ ___ ___   ___ ___ ___ ___

___ ___ ___ ___   ___ ___ ___ ___ ___ ___

Did you know this fact? _____

Did your grown-up know this fact? _____

17 ▶ Draw It

Follow the directions below.
When you finish, you will have a silly picture.

1. Draw a fish in the box.
2. Draw a tree next to the frog.
3. Draw a hat on the fish.
4. Draw a giant apple near the frog.
5. Draw a rainbow over the box.
6. Draw a flower beside the fish.
7. Draw potatoes under the tree.
8. Draw orange grass around the box.
9. Draw a balloon above the frog.

No Sillies Allowed

Play this game with a grown-up.
Make number cards like these.

1	2	3	4
5	6	7	8

Turn over the cards and mix them up.
Pick a card.
The number on the card tells you which words to use from the box.
Try to use the words to finish one of your sentences.
Write the words on the line.
If you can only make a silly sentence, turn the card back over and wait for your next turn.
Let your grown-up have a chance.
The first player to finish all 4 sentences wins.

1. in a house	4. in the drawer	7. near the fireplace
2. down the hill	5. on the pillow	8. between the chairs
3. under the bed	6. beside the shelf	

My Sentences

1. My shirt is _____.

2. I rode a bike _____.

3. The cat sleeps _____.

4. I live _____.

My Grown-up's Sentences

1. My shoe is _____.

2. The table is _____.

3. The wood is _____.

4. The book is _____.

18 › What's the Story?

"No matter what, I won't miss this game,"
thought Len as he grabbed his bat.

Is this sentence from an animal story, a sports story,

or a fairy tale? _____

Why do you think so? _____

_____

Draw a line to match each sentence with its story.

Jo wondered why Mrs. Murphy   Doctor Story
had a bowl of popcorn on the
roof of her house.

Rosa had never climbed a   Adventure Story
mountain before, but she
was not afraid.

Dr. Dove was tired after his   Funny Story
long day in the hospital.

Write one sentence for each kind of story.

Scary Story _____

_____

Travel Story _____

_____

Outer Space Story _____

_____

Sentence Fun

It is easy to make a sentence.
Just tell who—did what—when.

Who	Did What	When
George's cat	chased a mouse	this afternoon.

Who	Did What	When
The cook	made applesauce	for dinner.

Mix things up and you get funny sentences.

Who	Did What	When
George's cat	made applesauce	this afternoon.

Who	Did What	When
The cook	chased a mouse	for dinner.

Write a who—did what—when sentence.
Your grown-up must also write a sentence.
Then mix things up to make 2 funny sentences.

My Sentence

Who	Did What	When

My Grown-up's Sentence

Who	Did What	When

Funny Sentence 1

Who	Did What	When

Funny Sentence 2

Who	Did What	When

19 ▷ Who Did It?

Someone took a crunchy from the crunchy jar.
Who did it?
Follow the directions and you will find out.

1. Cross out anyone with curly hair.
2. Cross out the girl in a dress.
3. Circle anyone with a hat.
4. Circle Joe.
5. Cross out anyone with a book.

CARLOS   KIM   LEE   KAREEM   NEEMA   JOE

Whom did you cross out **and** circle? _____
You found the crunchy crook!

Make a Cat

Do this with a grown-up.
If you want to, make a whole family of cats.

1. Start with a square piece of paper.

2. Fold the square to make a triangle.

 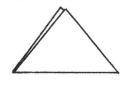

3. Fold the top point of the triangle down and forward.

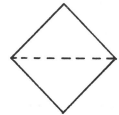 

4. Fold the bottom points up and forward.

5. Turn the paper around and draw a cat face.

20 ▷ Vacation Time

It is vacation time.
Some children are going away.
Jill is going skiing.
Paul is going to the seashore.
Ana is going to Washington, D.C.

Each child has a suitcase.
Each suitcase is packed.
Figure out who gets each suitcase.
Circle the right name.

Jill   Paul   Ana

Jill   Paul   Ana

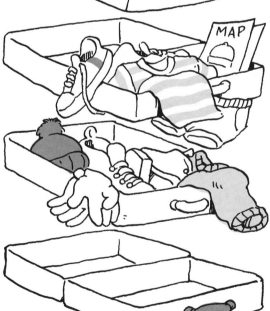

Jill   Paul   Ana

Pack a suitcase for a trip to
a cabin in the woods.
Write 3 things you will need.

_____

_____

_____

What's the Game?

Have a grown-up read these rules to you.

You need 2 players.
You play on a board that is covered with red and black squares.
One player uses round red pieces.
The other player uses round black pieces.
The pieces slide around the board.
Pieces can also jump.
Red pieces capture black pieces by jumping over them.
Black pieces capture red pieces by jumping over them.
You try to capture all the other player's pieces.

Can you name the game?

What is the game? _____

Here are the names of some games.

baseball   basketball   soccer

tic-tac-toe   hopscotch   chess

Choose one of the games.
Tell your grown-up how to play.
Do not say the name of the game.
Have your grown-up try to guess the name of the game.
Then let your grown-up explain a game.
You guess the name of the game.

My game was _____.

What game did your grown-up guess? _____

My grown-up's game was _____.

What game did you guess? _____

21 It's a Problem

Mike has a problem.

What will Mike do now?
Write your idea.

_____

_____

_____

_____

_____

_____

What Next?

Read this story with a grown-up.

Lola was running up the school steps. She was in a hurry. She had the lead part in her school play, and the show was about to start. Suddenly Lola tripped. She twisted her foot. It hurt a lot. Lola tried to walk, but her foot hurt too much.

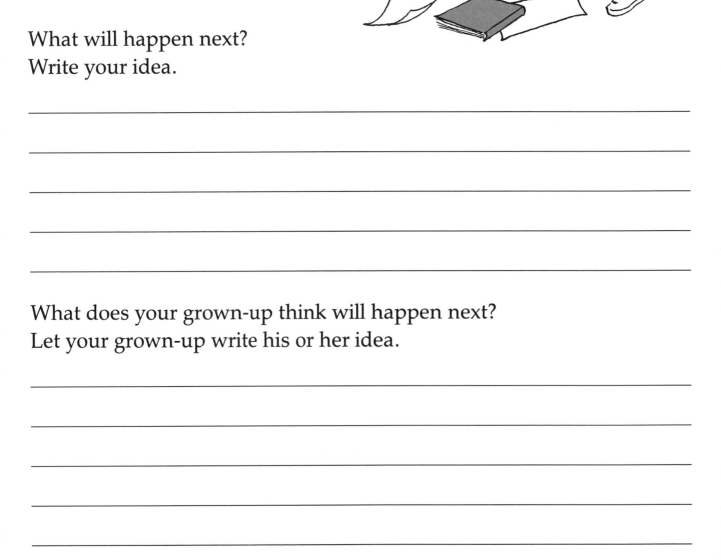

What will happen next?
Write your idea.

_____

_____

_____

_____

What does your grown-up think will happen next?
Let your grown-up write his or her idea.

_____

_____

_____

_____

22 ⟩ Birthday Party

Plan a birthday party.
You may invite 4 friends.
Write their names.

_____

_____

_____

_____

Decide on 4 special things to do for the party.
You may go bowling, go to the movies, invite
a magician, whatever you want.

First we will _____

_____

Second we will _____

_____

Third we will _____

_____

Fourth we will _____

_____

You will be given birthday gifts.
Write down 4 gifts you would like to have.

_____   _____

_____   _____

Before, During, After

Ask a grown-up to guess what you did today.
Your grown-up must guess something you did
before lunch, during lunch, and after lunch.
Have your grown-up write the guesses here.

Before lunch _____

During lunch _____

After lunch _____

Were your grown-up's guesses right?

Before lunch _____ During lunch _____ After lunch _____

Now it is your turn.
Guess what your grown-up did before lunch,
during lunch, and after lunch.
Write your guesses here.

Before lunch _____

_____

During lunch _____

_____

After lunch _____

_____

Were your guesses right?

Before lunch _____ During lunch _____ After lunch _____

23 ▷ Off to the Movies

Here is a movie poster.
It is filled with information.
Read the poster and then answer the questions.

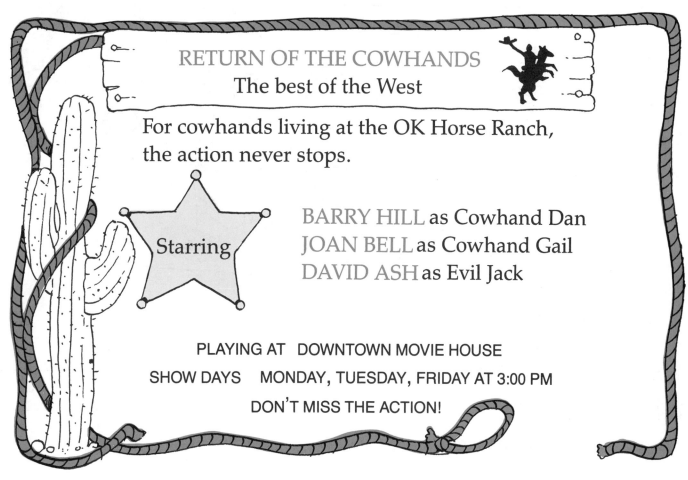

RETURN OF THE COWHANDS
The best of the West

For cowhands living at the OK Horse Ranch,
the action never stops.

Starring

BARRY HILL as Cowhand Dan
JOAN BELL as Cowhand Gail
DAVID ASH as Evil Jack

PLAYING AT   DOWNTOWN MOVIE HOUSE

SHOW DAYS   MONDAY, TUESDAY, FRIDAY AT 3:00 PM

DON'T MISS THE ACTION!

Tell about the movie.

What is the name of the movie? _____

Who plays Evil Jack? _____

Where do the cowhands live? _____

Can you see the show on Sunday? _____

What time is the show? _____

What Happened Here?

Look at this picture.
Work with a grown-up to answer the questions.
Try to find out what happened.

What time of day is it? _____

How do you know? _____

Why is the picnic basket open? _____

Why is the family upset? _____

Where is the picnic food? _____

What will the family do now? _____

Write a short story to go with the picture.
Tell the story to your grown-up.
Your grown-up will help you write your story.
Write your story on another sheet of paper.

Why? Why? Why?

It is hard to finish a story when Alvin is around.
That's because Alvin is always asking, "Why?"
In this story, when Alvin asks "Why," you write the answer.

Five Lemmots from the planet Lem make the
long trip from Lem to Earth.
Alvin asks, "Why?"   My answer is _____

_____

The Lemmots land on a farm. They see cows
eating grass. The Lemmots are surprised.
Alvin asks, "Why?"   My answer is _____

_____

The farmer, his wife, and their children see the
Lemmots, but they can't believe their eyes.
Alvin asks, "Why?"   My answer is _____

_____

The Lemmots act very friendly toward the people.
Alvin asks, "Why?"   My answer is _____

_____

The farmer and his wife invite the visitors to look
over the farm. The Lemmots stay a week.
Alvin asks, "Why?"   My answer is _____

_____

Finally, the Lemmots return home to Lem.
Alvin asks, "Why?"   My answer is _____

_____

What Will Happen?

Do this with a grown-up.
Read this story out loud to your grown-up.

Pam and Sam are twins. They are at home alone after school. They know they should not play ball in the living room, but they play anyway. They are having a great time. Then Pam throws the ball to Sam, but Sam misses it. The ball crashes into Mom's best red and white vase. The vase falls down. The vase smashes to bits. Water, a rose, and pieces of red and white vase cover the floor. What a mess!

What will happen next?
Write your idea here.
Tell your grown-up to write his or her idea on another paper.

_____

_____

_____

_____

_____

_____

25 ▷ Silly Nilly

Nilly is the silliest person in the world.
Help tell Nilly's story.
Fill in all the blanks and show just how silly Nilly
can be.

The Silliest Nilly in the World

Nilly is the silliest person in the world. One
day Nilly ate 500 lemons for lunch. Now, isn't
that silly?

On another day, Nilly _____

_____

Nilly's favorite games are _____

_____

Nilly hates it when _____

_____

Nilly loves to _____

_____

When it is time to go to school, Nilly always _____

_____

It was really funny when Nilly _____

_____

What a silly Nilly!

My Friend

Do this with a grown-up.
Some people make good friends.
Some people do not make good friends.
Here are some famous people.
Read each name.
Decide if you would like the person for a friend.
Write the reason you have this feeling.
Then let your grown-up decide.

Cinderella

Would you like Cinderella for a friend? _____

Why? _____

Would your grown-up like Cinderella for a friend? _____

Why? _____

Humpty-Dumpty

Would you like Humpty-Dumpty for a friend? _____

Why? _____

Would your grown-up like Humpty-Dumpty for a friend? _____

Why? _____

Hansel and Gretel

Would you like Hansel and Gretel for friends? _____

Why? _____

Would your grown-up like Hansel and Gretel for friends? _____

Why? _____

26 **Two Young People**

Here are two stories about real people.
Read the stories to find out something important about each person.

Helen Keller

Helen Keller could not see or hear. A wonderful teacher showed Helen how to talk with her fingers. It was hard to teach Helen. At first, Helen did not like her teacher. She did not know her teacher was there to help her. It took a long time, but Helen did learn to talk. She also learned to love her teacher.

What is the most important thing you learned about Helen Keller?

_____

_____

_____

Tell two more things you would like to learn about Helen Keller.

1. _____

_____

2. _____

_____

Louis Braille

Louis Braille was just 15 years old when he found a way to help blind people read words. Louis made an alphabet with raised dots. A blind person could feel the dots and read the words. The alphabet is named for Louis. It is called Braille. Louis knew how very important the alphabet was because he also was blind.

What is the most important thing you learned about Louis Braille?

_____

_____

_____

Tell two more things you would like to learn about Louis Braille.

1. _____

_____

2. _____

_____

Is It True?

Do this with a grown-up.
Read the three animal stories below.
Two of the stories are true. One story is not true.
Decide if a story is true or not true.
You and your grown-up will circle your answer choices.

Crabs protect themselves in a strange way. If an enemy grabs a crab by the leg, the crab lets its leg fall off. Later it grows a new leg.

I think this story is   true   not true
My grown-up thinks this story is   true   not true

Camels live in the desert and sometimes go without food for many days. The camel has a hump filled with fat. The camel lives off the fat in its hump until it can get more food.

I think this story is   true   not true
My grown-up thinks this story is   true   not true

The wood turtle crawls out of its shell to hunt for bugs that live in the trees. Then it goes back in its shell to eat the bugs.

I think this story is   true   not true
My grown-up thinks this story is   true   not true

Each sentence below tells about one of the animal stories.
If the sentence gives the main idea of the story, the story is true.
If the sentence does not give the main idea, the story is not true.

1. A crab will drop off a leg to protect itself.
2. Fat in a camel's hump helps keep it alive.
3. Turtles eat bugs.

27 ▷ Follow the Plan

Here are two story plans. Read them both.
Which plan do you like better?
On a sheet of paper, write a story to fit your favorite plan.

PLAN 1

What the story is about: Kate grows a flower. Her
        flower can talk. Her flower can do magic.

The problem: Kate wants to keep her magic flower
        a secret, but the flower talks and talks.

Important characters: Kate
                the flower
                Kate's teacher

An important fact: The flower grows legs and
        follows Kate to school.

PLAN 2

What the story is about: Fluzz is an elf who likes to
        tease. He lives in the kingdom of Muzz. Fluzz
        has been sleeping for 100 years. When he is
        asleep, all is well. When Fluzz wakes up, he
        begins to tease. Then everyone is unhappy.

The problem: Fluzz wakes up today.

Important characters: Fluzz
                the queen
                the princess

Two important facts: The princess is 7 years old.
                Fluzz loves to sing songs.

Odd or Even Story

Play with a grown-up.
Decide if you want to be odd or even for this game.
Read "Billy's Pet." Then look at the questions next to the story.
Circle every line that answers a question.
Add the numbers next to the lines you circled.
The sum will be either odd or even.
The player with the correct match, odd or even, wins.

Billy's Pet

Billy and his mom live in a small apartment. Sometimes Billy gets lonely. He knows a pet would make him feel better. A dog or a cat would be best. Billy asks his mom. Mom says, "Dogs and cats make me sneeze."

Mom suggests, "Let's go to the pet store. Maybe we can find an animal that won't make me sneeze."

When Billy and his mom get to the store, they see a turtle. The turtle looks at Billy. The turtle smiles. The turtle smiles at Mom. Mom sniffs the turtle. She doesn't sneeze. Billy and his mom shout, "A turtle is the pet for us!"

What is the story about?
Visiting a pet store   1
Choosing a pet   2
Living in an apartment   3

What are the problems?
Billy wants a pet   1
Mom hates dogs   4
Mom sneezes   3

Who are the characters?
A dog   2
Billy   1
Billy's mom   4

How was the problem solved?
Billy gets a dog   1
Billy gets a turtle   4
Mom is happy   3

Is the sum odd or even? _____

Who won? _____

28 ▸ The Truth

Sometimes writers make up stories.
Made-up stories are called **fiction**.
Other times writers tell true stories about things
that really happened.
True stories are called **nonfiction**.
Read and follow each direction below.
All the things you write will be nonfiction.

Tell three true things about how you look.

_____

_____

_____

Tell two more true things about yourself.

_____

_____

Tell three true things about your school.

_____

_____

_____

Tell two true things about a friend.

_____

_____

Interview

Find out some true things about your grown-up.
Read each question to your grown-up.
Tell your grown-up to give you
a true answer to each question.
Write down every answer.
They should all be true,
or **nonfiction**.

Where did you grow up?

_____

Did you live in a house or an apartment?

_____

Did you have any pets when you were growing up?

_____

What did you like about school?

_____

What didn't you like about school?

_____

What did you like to do out of school?

_____

What was your favorite food when you were growing up?

_____

When you were little, what did you want to be when you grew up?

_____

29 ▷ Goo or Roo?

Giants from the land of Goo say things that are true.
Giants from Roo say things that could never be true.
Read what each giant says.
Is the giant from Goo or Roo?
Circle your answer.

Last week I had a melted cheese sandwich.

I am from:

Goo   Roo

Yesterday your teacher flew to school on a bird.

I am from:

Goo   Roo

Tomorrow all the rivers on earth will turn to gold.

I am from:

Goo   Roo

Many children like to play with blocks.

I am from:

Goo   Roo

You can get books about monsters at the library.

I am from:

Goo   Roo

If you eat too many peas, you will turn green.

I am from:

Goo   Roo

Write something a giant from Goo might say.

_____

Write something a giant from Roo might say.

_____

Could It Be?

Do this with a grown-up.

Take turns.

Toss a coin.

If you get heads, cross out a sentence that could be true.

If you get tails, cross out a sentence that could not be true.

The first player who cannot find a sentence to cross out loses the game.

If all the sentences are crossed out, it is a tie game.

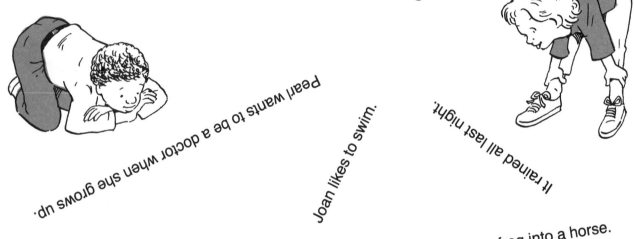

Pearl wants to be a doctor when she grows up.

Joan likes to swim.

It rained all last night.

Tim turns invisible when he eats oatmeal.

A robot turned Leon's frog into a horse.

Jim rode his bike to school.

It rained gold rings last night.

Keisha rang a bell and her chair started flying around the room.

Pablo likes to eat popcorn.

Earl's cat can talk Spanish.

Carmen went to live on the moon for a year.

Roberto did his homework after dinner.

Poems

Read these 4 poems.
Pick the one you like best.
Learn the poem by heart.
Be ready to say the poem in school.

First Snow
Snow makes whiteness where it falls.
The bushes look like popcorn-balls.
And places where I always play,
Look like somewhere else today.
                         Marie Louise Allen

On My Swing
Swoosh, swoosh,
Swinging high.
Wind in my hair;
Like the birds,
I can fly.
                         Peggy Kaye

To Bed
I don't want to go to bed.
I want more fun today.
But Mom says,
Tomorrow, tomorrow,
Tomorrow, tomorrow,
Will be the time for play.
                         Peggy Kaye

Toot! Toot!
A peanut sat on a railroad track,
His heart was all a-flutter;
The five-fifteen came rushing by—
Toot! Toot! Peanut butter!
                         Anonymous

Draw a picture to match the poem you like best.

Share a Wish

Do this with a grown-up.
You and your grown-up must finish this poem.
The poem does not have to rhyme.
Read each line and then write what you feel.
You finish each line that begins with ★.
Your grown-up must finish each line that begins with ★★★.

★★★ I wish I could _____

★ I wish I could _____

★★★ I wish I had _____

★ I wish I had _____

★★★ I wish I was _____

★ I wish I was _____

★★★ I wish that someday _____

★ I wish everybody _____

★★★ I wish for you _____

★ I wish for me _____

Draw a picture to match your poem.

31 ▶ A Magical Tale

Sometimes storytellers use their imaginations
to tell tales that could not be true.
A fairy tale is this kind of story.
Read the story and think about what makes it a fairy tale.

You are in a junk shop. You find an old, old jar.
You rub the jar and a magician pops out. The
magician says, "I will give you four wishes, but
only if you do a hard task."

You ask about the task. The magician says,
"You may choose the task you want. You may go
into the deepest cave on Earth and come back
with the lion who lives inside. Or you may swim
to the bottom of the sea and come back with the
King of the Sharks. Or you may go to the giant's
home and come back with a gold feather from a
magic bird."

Which task do you choose? _____

Why? _____

The magician says you may have anything you want
to help you with your task.

What do you ask for? _____

Why? _____

Pretend you did the task. What are your four wishes?
Write them down on another sheet of paper.
Tell why you wished for each one.

Fairy Tale Quiz

Work with a grown-up.
Take turns answering the questions in this fairy tale quiz.
Use RED to fill in the circles for your answers.
Use BLUE to fill in the circles for your grown-up's answers.
Check your answers.
The answers are upside down at the bottom of the page.
You get 10 points for every correct answer.

1. Who had a glass slipper?
Ⓐ Sleeping Beauty
Ⓑ Cinderella
Ⓒ A Billy Goat Gruff

2. Who huffed and puffed and blew down Little Pig's house?
Ⓐ The Big Pig
Ⓑ The Wolf
Ⓒ The North Wind

3. Who took food to Grandmother?
Ⓐ Red Riding Hood
Ⓑ The West Wind
Ⓒ The Giant

4. Who lived with the 7 dwarfs?
Ⓐ The 7 Elves
Ⓑ The Little Mermaid
Ⓒ Snow White

5. Who climbed the beanstalk?
Ⓐ Puss in Boots
Ⓑ Jane
Ⓒ Jack

6. Who ran away from the old woman and the old man?
Ⓐ The Three Little Pigs
Ⓑ The Gingerbread Boy
Ⓒ Rose White

7. Who helped the shoemaker?
Ⓐ Elves
Ⓑ The Giant
Ⓒ A Wolf

8. Who broke Baby Bear's chair?
Ⓐ Goldilocks
Ⓑ A Woman
Ⓒ Papa Bear

My score is _____ points.

My grown-up's score is _____ points.

ANSWERS

1. B 2. B 3. A 4. C
5. C 6. B 7. A 8. A

Practice your writing skills. Write your own plans.
Then write stories to fit your plans.

PLAN 1

What the story is about: _____

_____

The problem: _____

_____

Important characters: _____

_____

An important fact:_____

_____

PLAN 2

What the story is about:_____

_____

The problem: _____

_____

Important characters: _____

_____

Two important facts: _____

_____

Practice your writing skills.
Make up your own Tongue Twisters

Enrichment
MATH

Grades 1 & 2
Answer Key and Teaching Suggestions

AMERICAN EDUCATION PUBLISHING

MATH OVERVIEW

ENRICHMENT MATH was developed to provide children with additional opportunities to practice and review mathematical concepts and skills and to use these skills in the home. Children work individually on the first page of each lesson and then with family members on the second page. Every lesson presents high interest activities designed to heighten children's awareness of mathematical ideas and to enrich their understanding of those ideas.

ENRICHMENT MATH consists of 31 two page lessons for grade levels 1 and 2. At each grade level *ENRICHMENT MATH* covers all of the important topics of the traditional mathematics curriculum. Each lesson is filled with games, puzzles and other opportunities for exploring mathematical ideas.

AUTHORS

Peggy Kaye is the author of *Games For Math* and *Games for Reading*. She spent ten years as a classroom teacher in New York City public and private schools, and is today a private tutor in math and reading.

Carole Greenes is Professor of Mathematics at Boston University. She has taught mathematics and mathematics education for more than 20 years and is a former elementary school teacher. Dr. Greenes is the author of a K-8 basal math series and has also written for programs such as *Reach Program, Trivia Math* and the *TOPS-Problem.*

Linda Schulman is Professor of Mathematics at Lesley College . For the past 12 years, she has taught courses in mathematics and mathematics education. Prior to her work at the college level, Dr. Schulman taught elementary school. She is the author of a basal mathematics textbook as well as of other curriculum programs including *TOPS-Problem Solving Program, The Mathworks* and *How to Solve Story Problems.*

WHY ENRICHMENT MATH?

Enrichment and parental involvement are both crucial parts of children's education. More school systems are recognizing that this part of the educational process is crucial to school success. Enrichment activities give children the opportunity to practice basic skills and that encourages them to think mathematically. That's exactly the kind of opportunity children get when doing *ENRICHMENT MATH.*

One of the important goals of *ENRICHMENT MATH* is to increase children's involvement in mathematics and mathematical concepts. When children are involved in mathematics activities, they become more alert and receptive to learning. They understand more. They remember more. Games, puzzles, and "hands-on" activities that lead to mathematical discoveries are guaranteed to get children involved in mathematics. That's why such activities form the core of each *ENRICHMENT MATH* lesson.

Another important goal of *ENRICHMENT MATH* is to provide opportunities for parents to become involved in their children's education. Every *ENRICHMENT MATH* lesson has two parts. First, there is a lesson that the children do on their own. Second, there is a game or an activity that the child does with an adult. *ENRICHMENT MATH* doesn't ask parents to teach children. Instead the program asks parents to play math games and engage in interesting math activities with their children.

Published in 1996 by AMERICAN EDUCATION PUBLISHING
© 1991 SRA/McGraw-Hill

HOW TO USE ENRICHMENT MATH

Each *ENRICHMENT MATH* section consists of 31 lessons on perforated sheets. On the front of each sheet, there is an activity that the child completes independently. On the back there is a follow-up activity for the child to complete with an adult. These group activities include games, projects, puzzles, surveys and trivia quizzes. The front and back pages of a lesson focus on the same mathematical skill.

Activities may be done at the time the skills are being taught to provide additional practice, or used at a later date to maintain skill levels.

Within each level, the lessons are organized into four or five sections. These sections correspond to the major mathematical topics emphasized at the particular grade level. This means you can quickly locate a lesson on whatever topic you want at whatever level is appropriate for your child. Let's say your first-grader is working on addition in school. You can feel confident that the first several lessons in the addition and subtraction section will have something suited to your needs.

TEACHING SUGGESTIONS
Grade 1
Optional Activities

A TIP FOR SUCCESS

First graders will find *ENRICHMENT MATH* activities easy to understand. Each lesson has simple instructions and ample pictorial aides. Nevertheless, you may want to spend a few minutes explaining the lessons before having your child complete them. You might even play some of the games prior to giving your child the lessons. The games will liven up math time and prepare your child for success.

Part One: Counting and Place Value

ENRICHMENT MATH has 9 lessons on counting and place value. You can use the first lessons early in the school year. Wait to give the lessons at the end of this section, though, until your child is familiar with place value concepts.

Counting is the foundation on which children build all future math skills. The lessons in *ENRICHMENT MATH* help solidify this foundation. Doing these lessons, the youngsters will count knives, people in their family, doors, even sinks. Before doing the lessons, you can ask your child to estimate how many knives or doors they'll find at home. You can record the estimates and compare them later with the actual counts. After your child has finished these lessons, you'll have collected considerable data concerning your household. Try using this information to make bar graphs comparing sinks to doors and doors to people.

Here's another idea: take a counting tour of your home. Find out the number of coats in the closet, number of windows in your home, the number of pencils on Dad's desk. This activity can prime your child for the lessons, or make a good follow-up after counting at home.

A number of the lessons involve skip-counting by twos, fives, or tens. You can prepare your child for this with skip-counting contests. Challenge your child to clean up his or her bedroom before you count to sixty by twos or one hundred by tens. Be sure to count slowly.

Several lessons call for your child to count large collections (stars on a page, beans in a spoon). Try finding out the number of dried lima beans needed to fill a yogurt container. When the container is full, have your child count the beans one by one. After this, have your child take the same beans and group them by tens. Your child can record how many groups of ten there are and how many singles are left over. Compare the two kinds of counts. This will help your child understand place value.

Part Two: Addition and Subtraction

Children should have real objects to manipulate when they start adding and subtracting. That's why so many *ENRICHMENT MATH* lessons have children add sets of pennies or paper clips or draw pictures before solving problems.

The middle lessons in this section call for children to add and subtract without assigning concrete materials as aids. First graders, however, should feel free to use any counting tool they want, like fingers, beans, Unifix cubes, etc.

Some lessons in Part Two help children understand the commutative property of addition. Children who understand that 3 + 5 gives the same sum as 5 + 3 can memorize the addition table in half the time. A few lessons help children see the relationship between 3 + 5 = 8 and 8 - 5 = 3. Children who appreciate the connection between addition and subtraction have an easier time learning their subtraction facts. What's more, these children gain real insight into the intricacies of the number system.

Part Two is filled with games.

Part Three: Geometry and Measurement

Part Three is a grab bag of activities covering the major themes in first grade geometry and measurement curriculum. These lessons are well within the range of first graders, even at the beginning of the year.

When children share homework results, it increases their interest in the activities. After completing *What Rolls?* (page 50), for instance, your child might enjoy making a giant chart listing the things he or she rolled at home. Look in other places for more objects that roll. Add them to the chart.

Have a discussion about the difference between baby steps and giant steps or between grown-up steps and child steps. Try taking giant step measurements of your home. Can you tell from the count who has the longest stride?

Try *Your Hand* (page 56). Only this time have your child use two or three different objects to cover their hand drawings. Does the size of the object affect the results?

Part Four: Mathematical Thinking

In Part Four you'll find a variety of activities that help children think logically, observe patterns, develop spatial awareness, and discover the many roles numbers play in our lives. These activities aren't numerical or geometrical, but they do help first graders expand their mathematical abilities.

Since answers vary for Grade 1, there is no answer key.

TEACHING SUGGESTIONS
Grade 2
Optional Activities

A TIP FOR SUCCESS

Second graders should find the instructions in *ENRICHMENT MATH* easy to read and easy to follow. Even so, it's a good idea to spend a few minutes explaining each assignment. When children are familiar with the activities they are more likely to be successful. You might try playing some of the games before your child does them. The games should make a math time that is filled with fun and learning.

Part One: Counting and Place Value

There are eight lessons in this section. The first four help children count forwards, backwards, skip-count and order numbers from 1 to 100. Children will be able to handle these assignments even in the beginning of the school year. The remaining lessons help children understand the organizing principles of our number system.

There are many opportunities to expand on these lessons. After assigning *Numbers Everywhere* (page 77), make a chart of places you can find numbers at home.

After playing *Make a Number* (page 80), ask your child to figure out the highest possible score in the game. Did your child get that score?

After completing *Count by 10* (page 87), challenge your child to find other patterns on the 100 board. What happens when they count by threes, or fives, or fours?

Pennies and Dimes (page 89) prepares children to rename tens and ones by using money. After your child completes the lesson, record all the ways your child found to make 52 cents. Then have your child discover how many ways to make 82 cents with pennies and dimes.

Part Two: Addition and Subtraction

There are 100 basic addition and subtraction facts. We expect second graders to memorize them all. Memorization requires drill, but the drill can and should be fun. Games like those in *Enrichment Math* eliminate the dreariness.

Rote memorization isn't the only goal when it comes to basic facts. You want your child to understand numerical principles, too. Several of the *ENRICHMENT MATH* lessons help children develop this kind of mastery.

Don't hesitate to use these games.

Once your child has played plenty of games at home, have him or her invent their own addition and subtraction board games. You'll find that kids are natural game makers.

The last few lessons call for children to add and subtract three-digit numbers with renaming. Make sure your child is completely comfortable with this difficult skill before having him or her do the activities.

Part Three: Geometry and Measurement

Part Three offers you a wide variety of lessons covering most of the topics in the second grade geometry and measurement curriculum. Although there are only one or two activities on each topic, the lessons are effective because they give children "hands-on" experiences measuring length, weight, capacity and studying geometric shapes.

It's a good idea to continue the hands-on approach at home. Here are some suggestions. Have your child make a paper clip chain with 10 or 20 paper clips. Then have your child measure different objects in the room. How many paper clips long is your *ENRICHMENT MATH* book? How many paper clips long is your pencil? Try comparing the paper clip length with a centimeter ruler and an inch ruler. Have your child estimate before he or she measures. This will help your child internalize the length of a centimeter and of an inch.

Cooking will give children excellent opportunities to measure capacity. You can also have them weigh what they cook—either with a food scale or balance scale using both standard and nonstandard weights.

Part Four: Mathematical Thinking

Second graders must learn to think mathematically. They must learn to reason logically, to develop spatial awareness, and to observe mathematical patterns. The lessons in *Part Four* will help children with this part of their mathematical education. Children can handle these lessons even in the beginning of second grade. As the year progresses, however, children bring more sophistication to their work. This added sophistication will help children get more out of these assignments.

Since answers vary for Grade 2, there is no answer key.

Enrichment
READING

Grades 1 & 2
Answer Key and Teaching Suggestions

AMERICAN EDUCATION PUBLISHING

READING OVERVIEW

ENRICHMENT READING is designed to provide children with practice in reading and to increase their reading abilities. The major areas of reading instruction—word skills, vocabulary, study skills, comprehension, and literary forms—are covered as appropriate at each level.

ENRICHMENT READING provides a wide range of activities that target a variety of skills in each instructional area. The program is unique because it helps children expand their skills in playful ways with games, puzzles, riddles, contests, and stories. The high-interest activities are informative and fun to do.

Home involvement is important to any child's success in school. *ENRICHMENT READING* is the ideal vehicle for fostering home involvement. Every lesson provides specific opportunities for children to work with a parent, a family member, an adult, or a friend.

AUTHORS

Peggy Kaye, the author of *ENRICHMENT READING*, is also an author of *ENRICHMENT MATH* and the author of two parent/teacher resource books, *Games for Reading* and *Games for Math.* Currently, Ms. Kaye divides her time between writing books and tutoring students in reading and math. She has also taught for ten years in New York City public and private schools.

WRITERS

Timothy J. Baehr is a writer and editor of instructional materials on the elementary, secondary, and college levels. Mr. Baehr has also authored an award-winning column on bicycling and a resource book for writers of educational materials.

Cynthia Benjamin is a writer of reading instructional materials, television scripts, and original stories. Ms. Benjamin has also tutored students in reading at the New York University Reading Institute.

Russell Ginns is a writer and editor of materials for a children's science and nature magazine. Mr. Ginn's speciality is interactive materials, including games, puzzles, and quizzes.

WHY ENRICHMENT READING?

Enrichment and parental involvement are both crucial to children's success in school, and educators recognize the important role work done at home plays in the educational process. Enrichment activities give children opportunities to practice, apply, and expand their reading skills, while encouraging them to think while they read. *ENRICHMENT READING* offers exactly this kind of opportunity. Each lesson focuses on an important reading skill and involves children in active learning. Each lesson will entertain and delight children.

When children enjoy their lessons and are involved in the activities, they are naturally alert and receptive to learning. They understand more. They remember more. All children enjoy playing games, having contests, and solving puzzles. They like reading interesting stories, amusing stories, jokes, and riddles. Activities such as these get children involved in reading. This is why these kinds of activities form the core of *ENRICHMENT READING.*

Each lesson consists of two parts. Children complete the first part by themselves. The second part is completed together with a family member, an adult, or a friend.

ENRICHMENT READING activities do not require people at home to teach reading. Instead, the activities involve everyone in enjoyable reading games and interesting language experiences.

Published in 1995 by AMERICAN EDUCATION PUBLISHING
© 1991 SRA/McGraw-Hill

HOW TO USE HOMEWORK READING

Each *ENRICHMENT READING* section consists of 31 two-page lessons. Each page of a lesson is one assignment. Children complete the first page independently. They complete the second page with a family member, an adult, or a friend. The two pages of a lesson focus on the same reading skill or related skills.

Each level is organized into four or five units emphasizing the major areas of reading instruction appropriate to the level of the book. This means you will always have the right lesson available for the curriculum requirements of your child.

The *ENRICHMENT READING* lessons may be completed in any order. They may be used to provide practice at the same time skills are introduced at school, or they may be used to review skills at a later date.

The games and activities in *ENRICHMENT READING* are useful additions to any classroom or home reading program. Beginning on page 68 you will find additional suggestions for classroom games and activities to follow up on the *ENRICHMENT READING* lessons.

Beginning on page 283 you will find the Answer Key for *ENRICHMENT READING*. In many cases, your child's answers will vary according to his or her own thoughts, perceptions, and experiences. Always accept any reasonable answers your child gives.

Also available from American Education Publishing—

MASTER SKILLS SERIES SKILL BOOKS

The Master Skills Series is not just another workbook series. These full-color workbooks were designed by experts who understand the value of reinforcing basic skills! Subjects include Reading, Math, English, Comprehension, Spelling and Writing, and Thinking Skills.

• 88 pages   • 40 titles   • All-color   • $5.95 each

TEACHING SUGGESTIONS
Grade 1
Optional Activities

A TIP FOR SUCCESS

Beginning readers are sure to enjoy the activities, card games, board games, puzzles, and drawing activities in Level 1 of *ENRICHMENT READING*. The directions are straightforward and easy to understand, and there are ample pictorial aids. Nevertheless, you may want to spend a few minutes explaining the lessons to your child. Feel free to play the games and do the activities before assigning them. The games and activities will prepare students for success as well as make for enjoyable reading.

Readiness

The Readiness unit contains four lessons, two covering visual skills and two covering auditory skills. To begin, children work independently to match one clown drawing to another. This activity requires children to make visual comparisons between the two clowns. Then children play a modified lotto game in which they have to discriminate between different abstract patterns. Children also play a visual memory game and complete a simple maze. Most children love solving mazes, so you may want to supplement *To the Doghouse* (page 145) by making additional mazes for your child to solve. Children may also enjoy making their own simple mazes.

The lessons covering visual skills can help you evaluate your child's visual strengths and weaknesses. Children with good visual skills are likely to do well with a reading program that emphasizes a sight vocabulary and whole language approach. Children with less developed visual skills will probably do better with a reading program that also emphasizes phonics skills.

In the first lesson covering auditory skills, children identify rhyming words. Any number of additional rhyming activities, including reciting nursery rhymes and creating nonsense rhymes, may be used to supplement this page. Next, children play an auditory memory game in which they have to remember and follow directions. In the second lesson, they match the consonant sounds heard at the beginnings and endings of words.

The lessons covering auditory skills can help you evaluate the auditory strengths and weaknesses of students. Children who have trouble recognizing rhyming sounds, remembering what they hear, or matching beginning and ending sounds of words may have some difficulty with phonics skills. If you are aware of your child's individual needs, you will be able to adjust reading instruction accordingly.

Word Skills

The Word Skills unit contains eight lessons which cover basic consonant sound and vowel sound skills. There are lessons on initial and final consonants, consonant blends, consonant digraphs, short vowels, and long vowels formed by the addition of a silent *e*.

Beginning readers will be happy to participate in the playful approach to skills practice in these lessons. You may use the lessons to help your child practice skills he or she is just learning. You may use the lessons to review skills taught previously. Since children are eager to play games, and they are willing to play the same games over and over, the games offer a perfect way to help children master skills. Once your child is familiar with the games, you will be able to assign enjoyable word skills practice all year long.

After children complete *Silly Drawings* (page 157), try this game. Make nine playing cards, each with a different short vowel word on it. Then give each child a blank tic-tac-toe board and dictate the nine words. After you say each word, have the children write it in a box on their boards. They may write the words in any boxes they choose. Now mix the cards, draw one, and read the word on it aloud. Have the children look for the word on their boards and cross it out with an X. Then draw another card and repeat the procedure. Keep playing until one child gets tic-tac-toe. This child then says, "Tic, tac, toe," and wins the game.

Vocabulary

The Vocabulary unit contains six lessons designed to help children develop strong sight vocabularies and increase their general word knowledge. Children need to develop a store of words they can read at first sight. They also need to know how to use strategies other than phonic decoding to figure out new words. In fact, the fluent reader sounds out words selectively. What's more, many of the most common used English words do not follow regular phonetic rules.

Here are some suggested activities that may be used to complement the lessons in this unit. After your child completes *Like It or Not* (page 167), try making a list of your child's likes and dislikes. Tack two large sheets of chart paper onto a wall or bulletin board. Label one chart "I Like It." Label the other chart "I Do Not Like It." Help your child write things he or she likes and dislikes on the appropriate charts. Your child may make as many entries as she or he wants. You may also want to write some of your own likes and dislikes on the charts.

After your child completes *Label Me* (page 169), try putting labels on objects at home. Have a meeting to elicit names of objects in the room. Encourage your child to name less obvious objects, such as the doorknob, light switch, and pencil sharpener. Then have your child choose four or five of the objects named and write the name of each object on a card. Let your child tape each card on the appropriate object in the room. In a few days, repeat the activity. Soon you will have a fully labeled home or room.

Word Checkers (page 172) is also designed to help children develop their sight vocabularies. You may want to keep a supply of blank checkerboards available for your use. When the time is right, fill in the boxes with a selection of important sight words. Children will like playing the game, and you will like seeing how quickly their sight vocabularies grow.

Children who use context clues to figure out new words have a big reading advantage. These children decipher words as they read. In effect, they teach themselves to read. *A Riddle* (page 177) and *Lost Words* (page 178) will help children develop this important skill. If your child likes the approach used on these pages, it is easy to create similar activities for home use. You may also extend the lesson with a game called *Buzz*. Tell a story to your child. At selected moments in the story, say "buzz" instead of a word. For example, "Once there was a *buzz* child who lived in the big, dark woods." Have your child supply an appropriate word to replace *buzz*. Accept any reasonable choice, such as *little*, *big*, *silly*, *friendly*. Then continue the story.

Comprehension

The Comprehension unit contains ten lessons, each focusing on a different aspect of comprehension. To begin, children identify the main idea of a picture. Picture clues are very important to beginning readers, and they often use illustrations to derive meaning from text. After students complete *Name the Pictures* (page 179) and *What Is Happening?* (page 180), you may want to provide them with additional practice in finding the main idea of a picture. Use interesting pictures or photographs from your picture file, or clip some pictures from old magazines. Present the pictures to the children. Ask your child questions about the pictures in the manner of *What Is Happening?* Then encourage your child to make up titles that reflect the main ideas of the pictures.

A game called *Gotcha* may be used after your child completes Lessons 20 and 23. Describe to your child how to do a simple task, such as brushing your teeth or making a sandwich, but make one or more mistakes in the description. For example, you might change the sequence: "I put the toothbrush in my mouth and then I put toothpaste on the toothbrush." or you might add an inappropriate direction: "I put the toothbrush in my mouth and then I put on my shoes." Or you might leave out some important parts of the directions: "I went into the bathroom, got a tube of toothpaste, and brushed my teeth." Each time your child catches a mistake, he or she says "Gotcha!"

To help children understand the stories they read, they should be encouraged to think about relationships of events. One way to do this is to ask children to predict outcomes based on events in stories. You may ask your child to do this as he reads by himself. Help your child record ideas on prediction cards so he may compare his predictions with what actually happens in the stories. You may also ask your child to predict outcomes when you read aloud. Pick a good moment to stop and ask, "What do you think will happen next?" When you continue reading, compare the predictions with what actually happens.

Forms of Writing

The forms of Writing unit contains three lessons in which children are exposed to nonfiction, poetry, folk tales, and fairy tales. To complement these lessons, try to read a variety of nonfiction, poetry, folk tale, and fairy tale selections to your child.

Answer Key
Grade 1–Enrichment Reading

Level 1

Page 143 *Students draw:* tassel on hat, circles on hat, hair, facial markings, circles on suit, stripes on shoes

Page 144 Results will vary.

Page 145

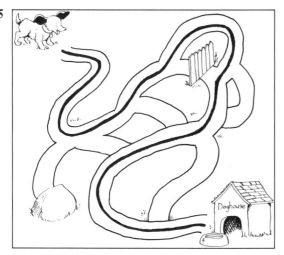

Page 146 Number of colored stars will vary.

Page 147 *Lines connect:* hat–bat–cat, boat–coat–goat, star–jar–car

Page 148 Answers will vary.

Page 149 *Circled letters:* y, e, s; yes

Page 150 Words and pictures will vary.

Page 151 *Possible blue:* farmer, fish, football, fan, fence, fox *Possible yellow:* dog, doghouse, door, dishes, duck, donkey *Possible red:* two tables, top, teapot, tomatoes, turtle

Page 152 *Mom:* mirror, map *Dad:* pajamas, pen *Pat:* bank, book *Bill:* ball, doll

Page 153 *Colored boxes:* fan, can, pin

Page 154 *Possible words:* lap, lip, dig, rib, cap, fan, fin, map

Page 155 *Circled words:* pan, mop, cap, six, pot, bib

s	i	x	m	c	p
v	k	i	p	a	o
m	o	p	a	p	t
b	i	b	n	c	a

Page 156 Words will vary.

Page 157 Drawings will vary.

Page 158 Results will vary.

Page 159 *Possible words:* black, block, blast, flip, flock, flag, clip, clack, clock; slab, slack, slip, slap, track, trip, trap, frog

Page 160 *Possible words:* block, blob, bless; slip, slap, slam, slob, slab, slick; clip, clock, clap, clam, club, click; flip, flock, flap, flub, flick; grip, gram, grab, grill, grub; drip, dram, drab, drill, dress; trip, trap, tram, trill, trick, tress; stock, stab, still, stub, stick

Page 161 *Colored boxes:* chair, shoe, thread, cheese, thumb, shovel, shell, 13, cherry, thermometer, check, ship, chalk, thimble, chain, thorns, chick, 30, shelf, shirt

Page 162 Winner will vary.

Page 163 *Colored pictures:* kite, cape, flute, bone, cane, mule, pine cone

Page 164 *Box 1:* bite, cape *Box 2:* tape, cute *Box 3:* hope, robe, ripe *Box 4:* fine, kite *Box 5:* pine, note, ride *Box 6:* Pete

Page 165 *New words:* pine, cute, made, dige, bite, note; Sue

Page 166 *Possible words:* game, gate, tame, tube, fame, fate, fine, dame, date, dice, dove, dine, came, cove, cube, name, nice, nine, state, stove

Page 167 Answers will vary.

Page 168 Results will vary.

Page 169 *Labeled items:* chair, rug, floor, toys, bed, wall, window

Page 170 Stories and answers will vary.

Page 171 Circled words, pictures, and answers will vary.

Page 172 Game of checkers will vary, but students should know all the words.

Page 173 *Crossed-out words:* sky, fish, house, goat, grass; answers will vary

Page 174 Answers will vary.

Page 175 *Circled sets:* fast/quick, talk/speak, see/look, keep/save; 4

Page 176 *Words with same meanings:* little–small, silly–funny, below–under *Words with opposite meanings:* happy–sad, on–off, more–less, nice–mean, up–down; winner will vary

Page 177 *Mystery number:* 9 *Mystery word:* cents; 9 cents

Page 178 up, tree, friend; Squirrel, sky, bed; hug, into, eyes, asleep

Page 179 *Top row:* A New Pup, The Party *Bottom row:* The Picnic, Turtle Time

Page 180 Answers will vary, but should indicate the main idea of the picture.

Page 181 Puppy projects will vary.

Page 182 Students should be able to pick up the ice cube with the thread.

Page 183 Answers will vary, but should be items needed by a doctor, carpenter, and teacher.

Page 184 Words will vary, but should belong in the categories.

Page 185 Ideas will vary, but should tell what the zoo keeper might do next.

Page 186 Answers will vary, but should be related to what is shown in the picture.

Page 187 Answers will vary.

Page 188 Story 4; 4

Page 189 Yes, No, No, Yes, Yes, answers will vary

Page 190 4, 2, 3, *Possible answers:* bears, truck, robot, ball, Tim Bear or a bear

Page 191 *Book plan:* underlined sentences 1 and 3 *Swim plan:* underlined sentences 1 and 2 *Cook plan:* underlined sentences 2 and 3 *Garden plan:* underlined sentences 1 and 3; $1 + 3 + 1 + 2 + 2 + 3 + 1 + 3 = 16$

Page 192 Answers will vary.

Page 193 Names of people will vary.

Page 194 Answers will vary.

Page 195 The sun makes the moon shine.

Page 196 *My Story:* Marta likes her sister *My Grown-up's Story:* Don likes to cook food.

Page 197 Students color picture on the right.

Page 198 Results will vary.

Page 199 Answers will vary.

Page 200 *Story 1:* Betsy Ross *Story 2:* Thurgood Marshall *Story 3:* Martha Washington *Story 4:* Thomas A. Edison

Page 201 Pictures will vary.

Page 202 Poem will vary.

Page 203 Answers will vary, but should reflect the moral "You have to work for something you want."

Page 204 Answers will vary.

TEACHING SUGGESTIONS
Grade 2
Optional Activities

A TIP FOR SUCCESS

Children using Grade 2 of *ENRICHMENT READING* will find the directions easy to read, understand, and follow. Even so, you may want to spend a few minutes explaining each lesson. You might also play some of the games and do some of the activities before asking your child to do them. Children are more likely to be successful with the lessons if they are familiar with them, and the games and activities will fill children's reading time with fun and learning.

Word Skills

The Word Skills unit contains eight lessons which cover consonant sounds, vowel sounds, and word endings. There are lessons on consonant blends, consonant digraphs, hard and soft *c* and *g*, short vowels, long vowels, vowel digraphs, r-controlled vowels, inflectional endings, and comparative endings.

There are five card and board games among the activities in this unit. Once your child knows how to play the games, you may want to use them to provide your child with extra word skills practice.

Here are some suggested activities that may be used to complement the lessons in this unit. After completing *Yes or No* (page 213), your child may enjoy making his or her own sheets of "yes or no" questions. Generate a list of words spelled with vowel digraphs and have your child write questions using those words. After your child completes *Hidden Words* (page 215), he may enjoy making his own puzzles. Provide your child with help as needed. You may then duplicate your child's puzzles and use them at home. When your child completes *Riddle Time* (page 217), encourage him or her to share the digraph riddles with the family. Also engage in some sharing after your child completes *Tongue Twisters* (page 218).

Vocabulary

The Vocabulary unit contains nine lessons designed to help children develop their vocabularies and increase their general word knowledge. Children using Grade 2 need to increase the number of words they can read at first sight. There are two lessons in this unit to help children increase their sight vocabularies. After your child completes *Tic-Tac-Toe Words* (page 226), you may want to create your own tic-tac-toe word games for your child to play at home. When your child completes *Word Road* (page 228), you may want to create a large version using words from pages 226 and 228 or other appropriate sight words.

Many young children have difficulty with compound words and contractions. The lessons on these types of words provide enjoyable practice that should help children master them. You may also like to create a compound word chart. Every time your child discovers a new compound word, he or she writes it on the chart. Aim for a chart listing 25, 50, 75, or even 100 compound words.

This unit also covers general vocabulary development. The stronger a child's vocabulary, the stronger the child's reading ability. An understanding of synonyms, antonyms, and multiple meaning words is crucial to the development of a strong vocabulary and reading ability.

Here are some suggested activities that may be used to complement this unit. A synonym/antonym game that is a variation of *Opposites* (page 236) can be played at home. Think of about thirty words children can easily match with synonyms and antonyms, and write each word on a card. Then make a two-section spinner. Write *opposite* in one section and *same* in the other section. To begin the game, have your child pick a card and spin the spinner. If the arrow lands on *same*, the child tries to think of as many synonyms as possible for the word on her or his card. If the arrow lands on *opposite*, the child tries to think of antonyms. The child scores one point for every synonym or antonym. This game may also be played by teams. Teammates must work together to think of as many words as they can.

Children as well as adults will get a good laugh from *Riddle-De-Day* (page 238). After your child completes the assignment, he or she may enjoy making a multiple meaning riddle collection. Every time your child hears or makes up a new multiple meaning riddle, he or she writes it on a file card. Keep the cards in a file box. Children will enjoy flipping through the cards for funny new riddles.

To extend Lesson 16, try this game. Write a simple, perhaps silly, sentence on a piece of paper. For example, "Tigers like to drink apple juice." Then read the sentence to your child, but replace the word *drink* with *beep*: "Tigers like to *beep* apple juice." Have students guess what word should replace *beep*. Several different words besides *drink* are possible, such as *make*, *swallow*, *sip*. Let your child keep guessing until he or she comes up with *drink*. Then the child may become the game leader. Help your child write a sentence and choose a word to replace with *beep*. Have the rest of the family guess until they come up with the child's missing word.

Comprehension

The Comprehension unit contains ten lessons, each focusing on a different important aspect of comprehension. To begin, children get practice in understanding the structure of sentences. *Sentence Fun* (page 244) is an excellent activity to help children write complete sentences. For additional practice, the activity may be done by groups of children. Encourage children to make their sentences as silly as they like. Children may also like to pick their favorite silly sentences and illustrate them.

Make a Cat (page 246) gives directions for making a simple origami figure. If your child shows an interest in origami, you can find books with suggestions for other simple figures in most libraries and many bookstores. You can also give your child additional practice in following directions with cooking activities. When your child prepares food from recipes, he or she must read and follow directions. As he cooks, your child will grow as a reader, and you will all get some tasty things to eat.

Predicting outcomes of events in stories is an important skill that helps children think about relationships of events. Children who can predict what might come next in a story usually read with more ease. Here is a variation on *It's a Problem* (page 249) that your child might enjoy. Cut out a comic strip from a newspaper. Then cut off the last frame and present the partial strip to your child. Read the partial comic strip aloud and encourage your child to come up with ideas for the final frame. Your child may even draw the frame. Then present the actual final frame and let your child compare his or her ideas with it.

If your child enjoys *Off to the Movies* (page 253), you may want to give this variation a try. Cut out a simple newspaper advertisement and make photocopies. Give your child a copy. Then ask detail questions that your child can answer only by studying the ad and locating details.

Cause-and-effect relationships are often hard for young readers to understand. After children complete Lesson 24, a game of *So I . . .* may be used to provide additional practice. Start by telling children a story: "I was walking to the park. Suddenly it began to rain, so I . . . " Have a volunteer finish the sentence. Then continue the story, having a child complete the sentence each time you say "so I."

After children complete *Silly Nilly* (page 257), give them a chance to read their creations out loud. Children will enjoy discovering all the different ways Nilly can be silly. You may also play a game of *Prove It*. Present your child with a type of character, such as the smartest person, the meanest person, or the strongest person, and have him or her write three statements that prove the character is indeed the smartest, meanest, or strongest.

In *Two Young People* (page 259), children read about Helen Keller and Louis Braille. Some children may be interested in finding out more about these two people. You can find easy-to-read biographies of Helen Keller and Louis Braille in most libraries. You might also read aloud to your child about these inspirational people.

After your child completes *Follow the Plan* (page 261), have him make up his own story plans. Provide help as needed.

Forms of Writing

The Forms of Writing unit contains four lessons that cover different literary forms. Children are introduced to the difference between fiction and nonfiction, and they get practice in distinguishing between reality and fantasy.

In *Poems* (page 267), children have the opportunity to memorize a short poem to recite at home. Before you give the lesson *Share a Wish* (page 268), make sure your child understand that not all poems rhyme. Young children can write excellent poetry if they feel free to forego rhymes in every line.

After completing *Fairy Tale Quiz* (page 270), some children may enjoy becoming storytellers. Each interested child may choose one of the fairy tales in the quiz, or some other favorite tale, and retell it in her or his own words to the rest of the family.

Answer Key
Grade 2–Enrichment Reading

Page 209 1 cot, 2 cut, 3 cat, 4 net, 5 hat, 6 pin, 7 pen; You are a winner!

Page 210 Words will vary.

Page 211 rice, stove, fire, Rose, Pete *Crime Report:* rice, five, Pete, Rose

Page 212 *Possible words:* kite, time, cape, mane, robe, tube, cute, fine, tape, note, loge

Page 213 Answers will vary.

Page 214 *Possible words:* seep, soap; toad; bait, beet, boat; beep; main, moan

Page 215 blue leaves on a pink tree; green grass in a tall glass; pictures will vary

Page 216 *Possible words:* trap, slap, snap, flap; grape; trim, grim, slim; trick, slick, stick, flick; grope, slope; slop, stop, flop; track, slack, stack, smack, snack, flack; stiff, sniff; smell; tram, gram, slam; trip, grip, slip, snip, flip

Page 217 *Riddle 1:* chair *Riddle 2:* chin *Riddle 3:* thumb *Riddle 4:* ship; riddles will vary

Page 218 Tongue twisters will vary.

Page 219 *Colored words:* spork, dirm, harb, larm, skird, flerp, sark, merm, lurst, slorp, chirff, lorp

Page 220 *Possible words:* barn, bark, park, part, stark, start; fork, form, corn, cork, stork, storm

Page 221 *Black:* case, cut, cat, call, color, camp, carry, across, second, carrot *Orange:* dice, since, race, cent, ice, fancy, mice, face, pencil, city, cell, place, nice *Blue:* will, party, room, pin, nap, tub, bath, orange, red, path, run, lift, add, wish, map; jack-o'-lantern

Page 222 Scores will vary.

Page 223 do*ing*, play*ing*, jump*ing*, eat*ing*; want*ed*; go*ing*, shout*ed*; stamp*ed*, watch*ing*, lick*ed*; get*ting*, scream*ed*, go*ing*; run*ning*, smack*ed*; hug*ged*

Page 224 Answers and pictures will vary.

Page 225 Answers will vary.

Page 226 Results will vary.

Page 227 Drawings will vary.

Page 228 Results and answers will vary.

Page 229 baseball, downtown, newspaper, lunchbox, notebook, armchair, sidewalk, sunshine, hilltop, goldfish, backyard, bathtub

Page 230 *Possible words:* toolbox, football, popcorn, airplane, airway, driveway, weekend, homework, fishhook, workweek

Page 231 *Lines between:* is not–isn't, we are–we're, he will–he'll; I will–I'll, have not–haven't, they will–they'll, could not–couldn't, that is–that's, did not–didn't; she is–she's, can not–can't, you are–you're

Page 232 Results will vary.

Page 233 *Red:* big/large, sad/unhappy, world/earth, road/street, thin/skinny, yell/shout *Blue:* gate/coat, door/rug, cat/dog, car/swing, fork/water, food/bed, spin/log

Page 234 Answers will vary.

Page 235 *Items with* ✔: 1. 2. 6. 7. 9. *Possible answers:* 3. well 4. far 5. low 8. cloudy, shady, snowy 10. early 11. old

Page 236 Results will vary.

Page 237 Turn on the *fan.* Open a *can* of beans. I need my baseball *bat.* I *can* buy that robot. The car must turn *left.* I need a *yard* of rope. How many apples are *left* on the plate? I worked hard and need to *rest.* Where are the *rest* of my toys? I am a rock-and-roll *fan.* A *bat* lives in a cave; yard; yes

Page 238 Answers will vary.

Page 239 Words and stories will vary.

Page 240 1. it 2. can 3. jump 4. over 5. four 6. people; it can jump over four people

Page 241 Pictures will vary, but items should be in these positions: fish–in box, tree–next to frog, hat–on fish, apple–near frog, rainbow–over box, flower–beside fish, potatoes–under tree, grass–around box, balloon–above frog

Page 42 Sentences will vary.

Page 243 sports story, reasons will vary; *First story:* Funny Story *Second story:* Adventure Story *Third story:* Doctor Story; sentences will vary

Page 244 Sentences will vary.

Page 245 *Crossed out:* Lee, Kareem, Neema, Joe *Circled:* Carlos, Joe *Crossed out and circled:* Joe

Page 246 Cat projects will vary.

Page 247 *First suitcase:* Paul *Second suitcase:* Ana *Third suitcase:* Jill; answers will vary

Page 248 checkers; answers will vary

Page 249 Answers will vary, but should indicate what might happen next in the story.

Page 250 Answers will vary, but should indicate what might happen next in the story.

Page 251 Answers will vary.

Page 252 Answers will vary.

Page 253 Return of the Cowhands, David Ash, OK Horse Ranch, no, 3:00 PM

Page 254 Answers and stories will vary, but should include details from the picture.

Page 255 Answers will vary.

Page 256 Ideas will vary, but should tell what might happen next in the story.

Page 257 Answers will vary.

Page 258 Answers will vary.

Page 259 Answers will vary, but should focus on Helen Keller's relationship to her teacher and Louis Braille's invention of the Braille alphabet.

Page 260 *First story:* true *Second story:* true *Third story:* not true

Page 261 Stories will vary.

Page 262 Choosing a pet; Billy wants a pet, Mom sneezes; Billy, Billy's mom; Billy gets a turtle; odd

Page 263 Answers will vary.

Page 264 Answers will vary.

Page 265 *Top row:* Goo, Roo, Roo *Bottom row:* Goo, Goo, Roo

Page 266 Results will vary.

Page 267 Pictures will vary.

Page 268 Poems and pictures will vary.

Page 269 Answers will vary.

Page 270 1. B 2. B 3. A 4. C 5. C 6. B 7. A 8. A

Also available from American Education Publishing—

COMPREHENSIVE CURRICULUM BASIC SKILLS

✔ **All the BASIC SKILLS for a complete school year!**

✔ **All COLOR LESSONS to help maintain student interest!**

✔ **EVALUATION of student progress is provided at regular intervals using Review Pages as Tests!**

✔ **The ANSWER KEY actually helps to teach! It is not just a listing of answers, but actually facilitates teaching by showing how the lesson is to be done!**